Contact

Shelley D. Chuchmuch B.ED, MAED, ED. LD (TBA)

311 Main Street Box 26
Angusville, Manitoba Canada R0J 0A0 PH – 204 – 773 - 2258
admin@shelleydchuchmuch.com

ABC-IQ® is a registered trademark™ of Shelley D. Chuchmuch
©2017. Shelley D. Chuchmuch. All Rights Reserved.

Other Shelley D. Chuchmuch Titles
Mind Science™ the Science of Health, Wealth, Happiness and Success

ABC-IQ®

What is truth?

What is culture?

Why do I have emotions?

What is energy?

How is energy created?

How is life experience created?

What is your intuition?

Why do I have tears?

IAM
"The strength of water
It cannot be shattered by a hammer or wounded by a knife,
The strongest sword in the world cannot scar my surface.
The waters of my river adapt themselves to whatever route proves possible but never forgets its objective:
THE SEA.
So fragile at its source, it gradually gathers its strength of the other rivers it encounters, and, after a certain point,
Its power is absolute". Author Unknown
Its power is TRUTH
I AM SENT TO HEAL YOU
I AM YOUR TEARS
I AM YOUR TRUTH

I CAN HEAL YOU POSITIVELY
AND
I CAN DESTROY YOU NEGATIVELY

CHOOSE YOUR ADVENTURE!
YOUR BODY IS A BATTERY AND A MAGNET – YOU WILL CALL ON ME THROUGH YOUR MIND AND YOUR FEELINGS IN YOUR CHEST.
I AM YOUR TRUTH
DEFINE YOURSELF!
YOU ARE UNFINISHED....YOU ARE UNWRITTEN....
I AM YOUR THOUGHTS....I AM YOUR EMOTIONS...
I AM ENERGY

For the worlds kids.

Shelley D. Chuchmuch

MY NAME IS SHELLEY DAWN CHUCHMUCH AND "I AM CANADIAN" a "BITCH" a "Pretty Woman", a "Steel Magnolia" a "Gambler" "Ask not what your country can do for you, ask what you can do for your country", "the Prophet" took the "Road Less Travelled" "North and South" and found that "Life is like a box of chocolates", "Invictus", you do know what you are going to get! "No Regrets", "It's Time", to "Breakaway", from "Dallas" , the "40 hour week" and the "9 to 5" I AM "Hidalgo" Let'er Buck! "! AHHHHHH relief! It's "Wonderful Tonight" "All Summer Long", Life in the "Finland Woods" "Country Roads" "Sixteen Candles" "Backdraft", "Hey Soul Sister", "Call Me Maybe" This "Brown Eyed Girl" destroyed the "Brick in the Wall" I "Silenced the Lambs" I AM "Love Actually" It was a "Blindside" by Tristan from "Legends of the Fall". I was hammered for being "The Messenger", "Cheech and Chong", "Mandala" "Robin Hood" & Good Will Hunting" so, I had a few "shots", turns out, I AM "Anna and the King" and I AM the "The Breakfast Club". "Mama Mia", "The Devil Wears Prada" and I learned "How to Lose a Guy in 10 days" As we crossed off the things to do on our "Bucket List" we studied "Sister Act", "the West Wing" And the" Shawshank Redemption" understanding 'The Man in the Iron Mask", "Boston Legal" the "Thorn birds" "the Godfather" and "the Newsroom", we had an "Awakening" I had some "Doubt", about "The Young Pope" and I had an epiphany, "Ocean's Thirteen", Its "The Perfect Storm", Learn from me Leonard, we aren't going to the mattresses! We are "Standing outside the Fire". "Release me"...From the "Titanic" I AM "Unwritten"! I AM "Aladdin" and "Cinderella", I AM a" Pocket Full of Sunshine" Let's dance the Lord of the Dance and Polka and "Raise Your Glass" "Fight Song" There is only "One Light...and One Sun"! "Everything grows" and I will "fix you" "I'd like to teach the World to sing"! "ODE TO JOY" and "O' Sole Mio" "and "Imagine" the "Claire de Lune" and everyone living in PEACE "Braveheart" show "Courage" think "the Sound of Music" Thank you for "the Ultimate Gift" Please "Pay it Forward" and show gratitude. "Cheers" What would you do if "today was your last day"? Thank you my "Friends". "Happy Days" Ahead "Celebrate Good Times" "I'm on top of the world" it's the "Best day of my life" "St. Elmo's fire" 'Oh, Happy Day" "OPRAH'S ON"! Think "Yes we can" be a "Rocket Man". "We Didn't Start the Fire". "We can handle the truth", I'm "kicking ass and taking names, playing my bongos on the beach"! I'm the Lincoln Lawyer, "Screw it, let's do it". It was the "summer of 69"! I don't chew my cabbage twice. I garden wearing gold. Thank you banker buddy,
"We are a family"
Thank you all for being a part of the opus of my life!
Thank you for creating the culture that is me!
Shelley Dawn Chuchmuch "Chuch"
"Hidalgo the Untamed Mustang"
Let'er Buck!

The Road Not Taken

Two roads diverged in a yellow wood,
And sorry I could not travel both,
And be one traveler, long I stood,
And I look down one as far as I could,
To where it bent in the undergrowth;
Then took the other, as just as fair,
And having perhaps the better claim,
Because it was grassy and wanted wear;
Though as for that the passing there,
Had worn them really about the same,
And both that morning equally lay,
In leaves no step had trodden black,
Oh, I kept the first for another day!
Yet knowing how may leads to way,
I doubted if I should ever come back,
I shall be telling this with a sigh,
Somewhere ages and ages hence:
Two roads diverged in a wood, and I-
I took, the one less travelled by,
And that has made all the difference.

Robert Frost

Table of Contents

Abstract Page 11
Author Prologue Page 13
Method and Materials Page 15
Results Page 17
Introduction E=ME2 Chapter 1 Page 19
The Problem Ed Re-design Chapter 2 Page 96
Policy Analysis – What going on in the world? Chapter 3 Page 118
Theoretical Physics Chapter 4 Page 133
The Law of Attraction Chapter 5 Page 136
E=MC2 Chapter 6 Page 137
VERITAS / Time– Judgement Page 151
Medical Science / Neuroscience / Positive Psychology Page 154
Sociology what is culture? Chapter 7 Page 156
Human Development Psychology Chapter 8 Page 160
Economics / Media – What feeds the mind? Page 163
Theology / Political Science Page 163
Conclusion Chapter 9 Page 172
Bibliography Page 179

About the Author Page 183

"What is past is prologue" William Shakespeare

I

AM

TRUTH

I AM VERITAS

I AM YOUR INTUITION

I do not speak language

I speak frequency

.....lalalalalalala

I AM ENERGY VIBRATION

Can you feel it? Can you hear me? What tune are you thinking?

TUNE INTO THE FREQUENCY OF JOY!

The Opus of My Life....The pursuit of VERITAS!

Let justice be done! To thine own self be true! TRUTH.

LOVE YOURSELF No one can bring you peace but yourself!

Happiness is totally an inside job! Rock on!

Dance with life and tune into joy!

When the Nazis came for the communists, I remained silent; I was not a communist. When they locked up the social democrats, I remained silent; I was not a social democrat. When they came for the trade unionists, I did not speak out; I was not a trade unionist. When they came for me, there was no one left to speak out.

Martin Niemoeller

Abstract

E=ME2 theory analyses systems thinking of culture providing a bridge of connection within the objective areas of scientific and medical research with the subjective, philosophical, sociological and theological areas of research creating a personalized system of global education delivered via technology supporting individual achievement in transitioning the frequency of the body from a negative to a positive state.

Foundations of thought for the E=ME2 theory are based on the law of attraction, which encompasses humans being pure positive energy. TRUTH or VERITAS, is emotional energy of the body and is vibration, energy, reading, intuition, truths, accurate, sensor.

This is human's judgement indicator. Intuition / energy is (TIME – Thought in Motion Eternally) which is a wiser "you "empowered by those that have gone before.

Love, gratitude and appreciation is the strongest energy igniting human beings with same powerful "GOD" force electrical energy that operates the universe.

This infinite intelligence energy guides through the thought and the emotions one feels to move forward to make choices in your life experience.

This energy operates you and the energy of the universe. This energy is either physically or non-physically focused. E=ME2 - Energy flows, where attention goes, experience grows! Energy is created from the mind and human emotion further creating life experience.

Through repeated patterns of thought, cultures of fear and sickness are being created. Negativity is the root cause of stress and sickness. The universe is inclusionary positive energy and always answers back with a YES to the thought and emotion request. Tears can heal positively as well as destroy negatively.

Author Note – Prologue

I do hope that this research inspires you and that you take away knowledge that you can apply to your own life experience to create cultures of success and responsibility in your own life.

However, in order to create cultures of success in your own life, one must take responsibility of the direction of their own life. Learn from my story, learn from my culture, for every bit of it is my truth!

In order to achieve your vision to complete your goals, you have to have a roadmap for how you are going to get there. In order to help you to where you are going, you have to know where you have been, however, one cannot move forward when their eyes are constantly focused on the past.

Knowing that, do you have a vision? What do you stand for? What do you really want to do? What's your story? What is your definition of life success and who sets your standard? How do you create the culture that is you?

This research is based on the Opus of My Life. It is my understanding of the world, as I have seen and experienced it. Know that I am neither a Liberal, Democrat, Republican nor NDP. I am many things, however, the Opus of My Life has been and will continue to be about the betterment people.

I view the world with the understanding that all people are human beings and are capable of achievement and that the only thing that separates us is culture and geography.

Please know, that I mean no disrespect to any person. I opened my life and thought sharing my experiences analysing everything that I held dear to me in the name of global education reform making large scale positive educational change.

In order to create solutions however, we must determine the root cause of the problem and extinguish it to implement long term lasting solutions creating change and cultures of responsibility.

Know that I come in peace. The world is my classroom, education is my religion, and humanity is my politics. With that in your minds. Let us begin.

Note Text" *Free Thought Research Journal"*

Method and Materials

Policy analysis of society determining the impact of global culture through travel to Africa, Asia, Middle East, and Europe, The United Kingdom and North America observing knowledge application skills based on the elements, influences and indicators of culture.

Eastern National Study 2006 – 2016. 500 students were assessed between the ages of 4 – 18. 50 female and 450 male nationals with 20 participants being non-nationals.

Each student was assessed determining grade level skill achievement and was also observed utilizing Blooms taxonomy of action verbs demonstrating knowledge application skills. Based on the result, personalized learning programs were created to fill in the "learning" gaps as demonstrated by every student.

Pre-Test Assessment

2% of the population demonstrated higher order thinking, knowledge application and problem solving skills. Students demonstrated "learned helplessness", lack of problem solving, planning, and transfer of basic skills.

Students also displayed a lack of ability to accept responsibility for individual mistakes, often resorting to the use of telling lies deflecting from the truth of the situation.

99% of students came from homes in which the "domestic help" played an active role in child rearing and all came from homes with excessive family wealth provided from the state.

Self-management and behaviour control strategies were more prevalent in the female populations. Male populations demonstrated far greater accountability issues, transfer of skills, issues with creativity and problem solving skills.

Post-Test

After one year of intervention and support being educated through personalized learning, 100% of the student population increased grade levels of achievement by 1 to 2 grade levels.

Children also demonstrated increased self-satisfaction, independence, organization and problem solving skills. Children also displayed controlled behaviour, self-management and forward planning skills.

Results
What is your vision? Begin with the End in Mind
New Subject Area –
Mind Science Positive Psychology
New system of education ABC-IQ® Global Management Systems©

The structure of programs at ABC-IQ® are applied skill based learning with students demonstrating understanding of Mind Science positive psychology across the disciplines through self-assessment.

This framework for education "franchise" includes Kindergarten, Private School Model, Policy and Procedures, Materials, Teacher Quality Standard, Assessment, Professional Development, K- 12 curriculum – in development and University programs accessible via technology.

We are currently conducting research on examining the impact of mind, neuroscience and alternative therapies on achievement in changing the tune of the frequency of the body from a negative to a positive state, **developing the** age 0 – adult skill curriculum via technology.

Note: *Author always wanted to be a Doctor (Ph.D.) holder but was not prepared to sit in a classroom to obtain degree. Based on applied self-directed learning - Created ABC-IQ Global Management Systems, a 21st century personalized system of global education delivered via technology, a new subject area of study Mind Science as well as The Currnie Chuchmuch Foundation INC and abc-iq learning platforms.*

Time – 2006 – 2017.

Chapter 1

Energy =Mind and Emotion - I AM the Singularity

What is education?
Do words teach or do we learn through life experience?

I AM here to give you a tune up! ☺ I AM going to give you a gift, a series of gifts actually, leading up to the ultimate gift, so, please, pay attention. I believe that this is one story you are not going to want to miss! In fact, it just might be one of the greatest stories of collective thought ever told!

My mission with telling you my story is not to make you think like me, rather, I just want you to think, to consider the possibilities. If today was your last day? How would you want history to remember you?

"I would like you to think of me as Dr. Feel Good. A prophet of the world's kids. An angel with tarnished wings with a whole lot of life experience. I am a BITCH actually. A babe in total control of herself! ☺

I AM Mother Earth, I AM Father Time, I AM Adam, I AM Eve, I AM Tesla, I AM Einstein, I AM IBN Khaldoun, I AM

Khalil Gibran, I AM Nellie McClung, I AM Joan of Arc, I AM Cinderella, I AM Aladdin, I AM Archimedes, I AM Aristotle, I AM John F. Kennedy, I AM Nelson Mandela, I AM Anne Frank, I AM Helen Keller, I AM Shakespeare and I AM Robert Frost, I AM William Ernest Henley, I AM Steve Jobs, I AM Mahatma Ghandi, I AM Elvis Presley, I AM John Lennon, I AM Luciano Pavarotti, I AM Robin Williams, I AM Van Goh, I AM Picasso, all rolled up into one! I AM TRUTH! As are you!

"My tongue at times can clip a hedge...and it has also been dipped in the sweetness of honey. I have experienced the greatest love and I have experienced the greatest loss. For every failure that I have had, I have had the equivalent success. There are two wolves in my chest that fight...the one that wins...is the one that I feed....deliberately!

However, everything is a process. When you know what you don't want, it brings you a lot closer to knowing what it is that you do want! But...the question remains...what do you really want?

Albert Einstein once said, "Everyone is a genius but if

you judge a fish on its ability to climb a tree, it will live its whole life believing it is stupid".

I AM a product of an education model that did not work for my style of learning. I spent many years fighting off a feeling of "not being good enough" because of my inability to read and write to the standard of other kids when I was young.

I questioned a lot of things, and some things, I just accepted because I didn't have the life experience to compare my thought to anything different.

Words did not teach me, applying words to my life experience did. I did not learn until I could apply the topic to my own life experience. Everything I learned in school prepared me for my profession but it did not prepare me for the trials and tribulations of everyday life.

In 2006, my entire life collapsed all around me. How did that happen? How could all of my worst night mares have come true? Was God out to get me? How could these experiences have entered into my reality?

My physical, mental, spiritual and emotional faculties

were challenged in a way that I had never been challenged before.

My entire body system was crying out for me to listen but I ignored the signs, life became something that I had to survive. I cried an awful lot, and for a very long time. What was the point of the buckets of tears I had cried and the stabbing pain that I had felt in my heart so often? Who created that for me? I had to intellectualize and understand my emotional pain. I set out to heal myself, I set out to find my truth.

My journey of seeking understanding truth has taken me from the physical, to the non-physical, to metaphysics, theoretical physics, spirituality, quantum physics, theology, philosophy, psychology, neuroscience, medical science, sociology, to history, to economics, to political science.

It has taken me from grief and despair to absolute joy, it has taken me from heaven to hell, to the America's, to Europe, to the United Kingdom, to The Middle East, to Africa and Asia, and it has taken me right back home where I started!

Great teachers force us to question. Great teachers force us to think, to seek understanding, to seek truth. Jesus, Mohamed, Buddha, Confucius, Abraham, Krishna and many others have taught us that there is something beyond all of us, but what is that energy, what is that truth? Where does it come from?

Was that energy that was something that was beyond me, or could I access this energy all the time? When we have the death experience are we finished or are we infinite?

Is there something that is waiting on the other side at the "Shawshank" that gave me my "redemption" that was waiting to put me on trial with the iron fist of judgement? **Was I really "HARAM" (forbidden) for that beautiful boy that stole my heart and turned my world upside down?**

Was I really going to go to "the mattresses" (HELL) if I didn't "follow" the rules? What was that whole process really about? No one has ever really connected the dots for me.

Theology teaches us that "**I AM**" created in the likeness of God, there is no death and that life is eternal. What does that really mean? Have you ever really thought about it? Most people tend to forget that part. *I have thought about this process a lot. Well, that and a whole lot of other things!*

"Like, who really did kill JFK? And seriously, did I really have to get down on my knees and ask for forgiveness for my sins? I may get down on my knees for a lot of things...

But......more on that later! What I learned is that nothing JUST happens. Like the domino effect, everything is inter-connected! One thing impacts another and everything impacts you!

I left Canada for my adventure in the east in August of 2001. It was a huge step for me to take. I had never traveled internationally before. All I knew, is I wanted to go!

The world awaited me. I had not done all that much traveling outside of the United States and Canada. All that I really knew was the culture of my community in

Manitoba and Alberta.

No-one really asks you why you believe what you believe. We have been raised from the grass roots to accept "*I said so*" from authority.

We never question rather we just accept things because this is what we were told. We don't really have a choice until one day, we break out of the chains of every day culture and travel.

Only then do we realize that maybe there really is more than one way to cut a cake. It may not be the way that we were taught but it serves the same purpose and achieves the same result.

I am one of those people who can honestly say, if I decided to continue my journey to the great beyond tomorrow, I would have…NO REGRETS!
…..why…because I know exactly where I am going…I understand the point of negativity and why we have it and I embrace it as learning!

I changed my perspective! I no longer see the word NO as a bad thing for NO just means…NEXT OPPORTUNITY! I no longer live in FEAR, for fear is just "FALSE EVIDENCE

APPERING REAL" Susan Jeffers...or...depending on your perspective...it could mean..."fu$& everything and run"!

We live in a world of polarities, we cannot live in a world without it. Universal laws are laws... no matter where you go on the planet!

If you knew that there was nothing that you could not do, or be or have, what kind of life experience would you choose to create? What is your muse? What tunes are you singing in the privacy in your own mind?

Are you singing positive tunes or negative? Are you playing the songs where you lose the farm...wa wa wa.... or the songs where you are inspired to take over the world? Woop woop! Is your world a wonderful place to live in or is it a shitty place to live in?

Whose version of the truth are you living? Who's thought, sounds, music and pictures are you influenced by? What words resonate with you? How do you create the culture that is you! What book formulated the foundation of your thoughts? What makes your heart truly sing?

Do you paint, sing, dance or play a musical instrument?

Do you plant the field, heal the sick or teach a child? Do you drill the oil, bake the bread, cut the hair or feed the people? Do you run the school or the restaurant, the company, office or bank?

Who or what cause inspires you to move forward? Why do you make the choices that you do? Have you ever really stopped and asked yourself who you really are and how you have come to be in the place that you are?

What sacrifices would you make in the name of success of your business or to achieve your dreams? What price would you pay to achieve your goals?

"With any situation, begin with the end in mind. But what is your vision? I talk about my goals with my council table...and I share my goals for a variety of reasons...someone might be looking for the same things as you and you can share knowledge...but also for accountability.

As everything begins with a vision. I developed well over 75 vision boards and lined them up down my street to connect the logic of the pieces of my story together.

I knew where I wanted to go, I knew what I wanted to

do and now I needed to put the pieces together of how I was going to get there. I worked on the research and development of my education system for 11 years for 15 hours a day 6 days a week without a paycheck.

I worked from my home based business, on the other side of the world, in a completely foreign environment, as a single woman, educating 500 children and consulting from my living room while developing this research further brining it home to Canada.

I literally sold off everything I owned! I survived heartbreak, broken bones, blackmail, empty bank accounts, phones tapped and emails hacked!

I was kicked, punched, slapped, spit on, called a dog and an infidel! And that was the tip of the iceberg...but there were phenomenal things that happened too. Otherwise I would have never lived in the Middle East for 15 years. It was an unbelievable magic carpet ride!

For every hour that you spend planning, will bring your eventual returns. My companies and dreams are like everyone's and are a work in progress....so...beginning with the end in mind...while finding the feeling place of already having achieved my goal. I worked smarter and not harder with the end goal of freedom 55, while building a life that I don't need a vacation from doing what I loved the most!

Knowing that education re-design is desperately needed and that information once it is produced in book form, becomes residual income and knowing that I wanted to obtain an inter-disciplinary doctorate, I organized my information for multiple uses, across a variety of platforms to ensure a global reach.

So, who or what do you look for your inspiration? Me....

"I am a lot like Steve Jobs. Like him, I shot a few people in the process of developing my innovation. It was not my intention, but in life, we know things happen and nothing comes without hardship.

I chose many business people who inspired me with what they had done with their business. I wanted to learn from the reality of my environment, learning from those who had boldly gone where I wanted to go.

So I studied the likes of Richard Branson's Virgin Group, Apple, Oprah Winfrey, Facebook, Google, Amazon, LinkedIn, Microsoft, Samsung, Ali Baba Group, the Bill and Melinda Gates Foundation, the Ford Foundation and the Kennedy Foundations to name a few. What amazing work these organizations were doing and how they were giving back to their global communities".

When I wanted to learn about business and franchises' I studied the values of my locally inspired Canadian leaders, Arlene Dickinson and I also looked to Jim Treliving and the Boston Pizza franchise business structures.

I looked to the Richardson's and what amazing contributions this organization had made to Canada and how they diversify their portfolios. I looked at Tim Hortons, Molson Canadian, The Four Seasons, Bombardier and then expended to the McDonald's and KFC franchises.

I examined global education models, national models and provincial models and focused on the International Baccalaureate as my standard. I learned from those that have gone before me and emulated what they did, however, building my own ABC-IQ® educational brand.

When I wanted to know about Universities, I looked to

the universities that provided the knowledge that I needed for what I was needing to develop the aspects of my research. Harvard Graduate School of Education in the United States was phenomenal for supporting with coursework through Leading Education Systems at the National Level for me to understand and develop my education system for integration into national education systems and University of California Berkeley on the east coast in California, U.S.A, to formulate my thinking about the Science of Happiness.

I examined programs at Cambridge and Oxford in the UK to see how countries handled their Ph.D. programs as well as other education models in Germany, the Netherlands, the Middle East and of course to Canada.

So, why do we do it? Owning your own business is a huge responsibility. Why do we take that on? Is it for the charge? Is it for the challenge? Is it for the FREEDOM? Why do we set any goal? Why do we do anything in life?

When that sense of competition is instilled in us when we find what we truly love as people in our businesses or in our own lives, we know what it feels like to be successful at something. We also know the feeling of failure. Only when you can feel the difference will understand and achieve success.

When you know the feeling of poverty, only then will you appreciate financial wealth. But how does one truly valuate how much something truly means? How do you put a price on your time, commitment and knowledge? How do you put a price on your "sweat equity"? How does one valuate their entire life's work?

How does one valuate buckets of tears, pain, hardship and the growth and knowledge that came as a result? What is my hardship and my life worth? What is my joy worth? Can you put a price on it? Can you put a price on love? What is the price of true knowledge and what would you to do obtain it?

I experienced the best time of my life living in the east, and I experienced the worst time of my life. Living in the east stretched my thinking and my understanding of the planet in ways that I could have never imagined.

I would highly recommend international travel and living to anyone. It is the only way a person ever really understands. It opens your mind, perspective and challenges you to get in touch with yourself as a human being. It changed the entire course of my life.

The eastern people reminded me. *"While you were judging others, oops, you left your closet door wide open and a bunch of skeletons fell out! Not everything is always as it seems however, everything is most certainly always interconnected.*

In the east, I met the Devil and I also met God! I found out what truth really was and in so many different dimensions"!

September 2001 – "we're going to smok'em out"

"I arrived to the east 2 weeks before September 11, 2001. Up until then, I had never heard of "Osama Bin Laden". Politics never really played much of a role in my life. I never had much of an interest.

That totally changed when I moved to the east and I saw what was really going on. How UN informed I have been as a westerner.

It was quite an experience to be in a room with people in

both the east and the west who had lost family as a result of what happened at the world trade center. That day totally changed the energy of our planet and would impact the global societal thought negatively for a number of years to come.

I can tell you, in all of my western programming, it could have never prepared me for what I experienced in the east. If the people of the west had to live each and every day under the same legal structures and negative cultural conditions as the people east, they could not survive".

I was brought to the Middle East to support with the establishment of a school for children with varied learning needs. This little country was just starting to begin the economic explosion.

It was amazing to witness history being made each and every day. The growth of this little country in such a short time was short of amazing to witness.

I am grateful to have been a part of the development of this country. It was exciting times to witness the positive. It was exciting to get all of the fantastic opportunities to travel, experience new culture, meet new people, eat new food, explore the planet and learn from some new books! Like everything however, every society and every situation has both positive and negative polarities and dimensions.

I walked into a completely empty classroom in September 2001. I had a few desks and that was about the extent of it. My first week I had a class of 3 of the sweetest kids that had the biggest brown eyes that I had ever seen! Eventually the rest of my class rolled in and I was introduced to the reality of my environment.

All kids still sweet, but this lot was extremely naughty! What was this about? What was really going on here? An 8 year old that has a Porsche, every kid had a nanny, driver, cook and housekeeper?

Pinch me, have I just landed on another planet? By the end of that week, I greeted my students by saying, good morning, I am your teacher! Leave your title at the door!

November 2005

"Giving the countries next young "leadership" a tune up:

Me: "You do not belong in this school. You are only here because you are not respecting the rules of the school and you are acting like, and I apologize and mean no disrespect, because I have never used this language before with a student in my entire career but...you are being... an "a$& hole"!

You are the countries next leadership! I am 100% certain that your father and mother would not allow you to behave and disrespect people in that manner! You are so much smarter and better than this!

Student reply: I am going to tell my father what "you", said! I said, to him, "go on right ahead, in fact, I would like to meet him and have a word about "your" behavior! Bring it on"! (His father was at that time, the "Emir of the country")

He went home and told dad. Dad's reply, your teacher is smart. Listen to her! That student left the school at the end of June. He went on to a school for mainstreamed children and then went on to University in the United Kingdom. He does not know it yet but I think that "tune up" was a life changer!

He is rocking it today! He always had the heart of a king! He just needed a little reminding about the realities of life. I have the greatest respect for his father. So I tuned up his little one because he was busy putting the country on the map and taking care of everyone else in the country.

So I treated his kin...like I would treat my own....well...his children...and the 500 other kids I would teach in the next 10 years"...

I worked in this position from 2001 – 2006. I taught a lot of great kids and met a lot of great teachers and heads of schools. *"I also met a lot of nasty teachers and nasty heads of schools that had zero vision or clue on how to run schools.*

Interesting thing however, the administration may not have understood my teaching methods but they certainly knew enough to bring every dignitary through my classroom door to have a peek at how I was delivering education in my classroom"

"Over the years my classroom was visited by the leadership of Qatar, Jordan, Spain and Kuwait. I also

had the opportunity to meet with leadership and discuss the needs of "special education". It was monumental for me as an educator to have had the opportunity to discuss education with these very progressive thinkers. It was an honor to have met them all".

2005-2006

In the end, with the "administration" of this school, it was not about doing what was best for students and our visions were no longer a match and we parted ways. Although, not entirely easily!

The "Kafala" sponsorship system would not allow me free movement and I had to find a "sponsor" with a "family name" that was influential enough that just by looking at it, the administration would have no choice but to "release me".

"Thank God for that fellow Canuck! He had my back during that terrible time in the school. He could see that I was being railroaded! As did a wonderful Irish educator. Thank God that angel walked into my life at that time.

I will never forget that day I met her. She came to our

school to teach us how to "Irish dance". I have this lady to thank for my supporting me through my darkest times in the country. We would work together over the coming years, solving the problems of the world, the meaning of the 10 foot wall around us and the impact of systems thinking on a global scale. This lady truly, gardens wearing gold!

At that time, my life collapsed around me. I had felt that I had hit rock bottom. My "fella" was with me one day, and went home to Jordan the next. His family married him off to a cousin I think. That scene did not end well for us both. He ended up divorcing not long after.

Although, hind sight is always 20 / 20. It wasn't much of a shock that he did that now that I know how he communicated. However, that whole scene left me in a very messy emotional and mental state.

It would take a number of years for me to heal and to understand. I can see that I suffered from a severe case of PTSD (Post Traumatic Stress Disorder) for many years after.

I do not want to re-tell the negative story because I do

not want to re-live it! Some thought is better left in the past. However, this story would not have been complete, as this was the reason this project began. I needed to mend my broken heart.

I had a breakdown on the other side of the world and I put myself back together piece by piece trying to understand why that happened.

I experienced my version of heaven and hell – love and hate. I went from living with anxiety that was masked as a heart attack to healing myself through the use of positive psychology and neuroscience methods of color therapy, meditation, neuroscience programs, massage therapies, hydrotherapy, Ayurveda, therapies, sensory, biofeedback therapies and medical marijuana (where legally available) in retraining the frequency of my brain and the energy in my body from negative to positive. What I learned through healing myself, I taught to others and developed this system of education.

Now that I have found the solution and have reached acceptance…I shall end that chapter of the opus of my life with, "it certainly was wonderful tonight". The bear inside of my chest is quiet. I am at peace. Thank you for the experience.

I graduated in 2006 as a result of my thesis, The Impacts of Education and Modernization on the Arab Muslim World from Michigan State University in the United States of America.

In that work I examined societies east and west focusing on eastern thought process examining what culture was being taken from the west, integrated into the east and why it was or was not working.

I read the most popular religious books, the Bible, Quran, Buddha, Confucius, Torah, Krishna and visited religious shrines in Kenya, India and Sri Lanka seeking the commonality of humanity.

Try as I might but I could not assimilate any of the language written in much of the religious text that was written based on the environments that existed thousands of years ago.

The "books" did not provide me the meaning of my emotions and did not provide me tangible solutions to questions that I had for my entire life about Theology. Why did I have these emotions? What were their purpose? I did not find my answers.

So, I continued my search for truth...Theology lead to Vedic astrology, astrology and then astronomy and eventually lead me to the Law of Attraction.

I also began a consulting practice from my home. I turned my living room into a classroom and began to teach those that needed help. On the 26th of December 2006, I also made the decision that I would develop private education.

There, in began my journey of seeking the resources one needs to establish a private school in the country. I was on a mission to establish a Canadian school.

As time as evolved and situations change, this project evolved into a paperless system of global education, however, it did not start out that way.

"My journey seeking funds and resources to develop Canadian private education continued. I worked on the business aspect in the morning and taught students in the afternoon.

I met a Persian man who took me under his wing and

introduced me to the hand's on learning I needed to understand "corporate and eastern business".

Between he, and a hand full of other people who I met along the way from my Canadian and Pakistani friends in the healthcare field to the Irish, American, British, Scottish, Australian, Egyptian, Omani, Emirati, Palestinian, Iraqi, Sudani, French, South African, Saudi and Jordanian educators, to the Qatari parents, children and multi cultured business men that helped to create the culture that is now me. Everyone had a hand in the influence over my thought and impacted my thought culture".

It is interesting, in Canada, if I described a person in this manner, it would be considered very "un-Canadian" and it would be classified as "racism". For me, I think I should acknowledge my history.

I am a Canadian. I am also Ukrainian and I am Polish. Interesting how we think it is not cool to label nationality but yet we label every other level of society. Black, white, people of color, lesbians, gays, straight, bi-sexual, transgender, left wing, right wing, high class, middle class, lower class.

"WTF? All these labels to separate and divide us and classify us as human beings! We are all people! We all have heads, we all have bodies, we all think and we all feel! Everyone tastes like chicken to a bear"!

"I did not have much experience with eastern business. I spent most of my time up until that point in a classroom. This man mentored me for a number of years, teaching me what he could.

Putting me in situations that I just would never think to put myself into. From chambers of commerce, to government offices, to embassies, to universities, banks and so on.

I was the first Canadian to enter the Chamber of Commerce. The most memorable perhaps was when I was invited to sit among the local men at a business forum.

April 2011

There I was "sitting in the first three rows of the forum were 200 men dressed in a sea of white wearing their cultural "dress" (Thobes) and me being the only female, dressed in a black business "suit". A moment I will never forget. This moment epitomizes my entire life in one picture!

It would seem that I was born to stand out. I quietly leaned over to my mentor and said, "We aren't going to get kicked out of here are we"? He quietly assured me as he always did with a gentle smile, nod or touch to assure me, no worries, I got your back; you are good to go! That was the day that I knew ... he was the one!

"It took me years to find this man. After meeting on average of 450 local people, I knew that "yes", this is the man that I need! He set the standard of excellence for every other business person that I met in the region.

I loved his energy and he made my heart sing! He was the perfect reflection of past, present and future in thought. He was opposite of me in every way possible. I needed a mentor who was kind, gentle and patient enough with me to understand my motivations and who could be open enough to give me their perspective.

He thought of me as an "alien". I thought of him as "Robin Hood". I think I fascinated him. I am pretty sure he hadn't met anyone quite like me before. Over the *years, I found myself saying things just for the shock value to see what I could do and how far I could really go!*

I should have taken up a job working a NASA because I certainly was being a bit of a "button pusher"! That expression used to make me laugh. We used to wonder what those boys did all day long at NASA....

I asked him once if I could come with him to an all "male" wedding. I wanted to see what went on there. It was like a "boys" club and I wanted to know what those boys did! I knew very well that I could not go, but I wanted the reaction! I loved hearing him laugh right out loud!

For me, it was music to my ears. On a rare occasion did I ever see him lose any composure or wear clothing outside of his cultural dress, so, just to be a pain in the backside, for the first 4 years that I knew him, I made sure that I wore a different outfit every time he saw me. Just so that I could teach him...I can wear what I want and still be me...Its ok to lose the "thobe" once in a while. Let's see you express yourself and show me your threads! I want to know YOU!☺ Not the version of yourself that you present to the outside world!

I needed a man who I could not knock over with my directness and one who would push me and challenge me right back!

Communication in the east is not so much about words as it is about body language. I am like the Kenny Rogers song the" Gambler" in that respect, but I think my mentor learned over the years...I too played to win!

Like the Hallmark card read, "treat me like a queen, and I will treat you like a king, treat me like a game, and I will show you how it's played"!

I wanted to experience his "male" world. I wasn't all that interested in what the ladies in the country were doing. I already knew...I wanted to play with the "big dogs". I had never experienced that kind of culture before.

I was used to the "nose bleed section and the "cheap seats". I loved to visit him at his work. I would drop in to enjoy the view!

I could never understand why he would sit with his back

to the sea? What a view of God's paint for inspiration! Hmmm...but...he did have one big massive desk!

As most powerful men did! I used to joke about the "energy" of the place in which he worked. I would come into his office and say, it feels very male in this building! So many big desks!

I would scale every detail of his office. The heavy mahogany desks, cabinets and the white leather furniture. Diamond awards, trophies and business magazines.

Taking in the scent of the "coffee" mixed with the smell of expensive cologne. The sound of phones ringing, land cruisers, BMW's and every other top name brand car driving down the road out the window.

To me, it felt like I was on Wall Street in the East. A whole new world! I loved the sound of his voice as it brought me a sense of calm when I heard it. His energy brought me power. His eyes danced! I could see, I brought him joy too! I loved learning with him as much as he loved learning with me.

I was a good protégé and he was a total gentleman! I

think he loved my attitude, I may be down, but I am not down for the count! "A quitter never wins and a winner never quits" Napoleon Hill! I am going for "platinum"! The best deal possible and I won't quit until I get it!

It was a joy to watch him work and he was fun to try to emulate! It was great to meet his extended family. They gave me courage to take a stand for what I believe and they tried their best to teach me how to convey that in a way that would not offend. They gave me the name "Mandala" and taught me how to say it with "honey". ☺

It felt great to be a part of that family. I fell in love with all of them. For me, they represented the family that I had left behind in Canada. I loved being with them but I cried every time after. "My uterus would feel like it was going to explode".

How I longed for the stability and the security of a "significant other" to face the world with. I was beginning to grow very tired of having to stand on my own two feet as the lone ranger all of the time. I had missed the solidarity of my family.

I think this is why I understood eastern family values. My family was not much different...but we just didn't share bank accounts...I was used to that kind of together ness...and I was longing for it... the feeling that no matter what, someone has your back!

The universe sends one what they need when they least expect it. One just has to be aware of what the universe is trying to tell you.

It's hard to hold onto the belief that success is in the journey when you are in standing up to your chin in excrement...what can you do in those times?? DON'T MAKE WAVES!

However....I can tell you it doesn't feel so successful when you hit rock bottom...the ride is a little rough during those times... but knowing how life tends to roll out...the negative does not stay that way forever...the situation will change when you can change your patterns of thought to experience success... some patterns...are very long standing...however, your integrity is everything!

A tip: If you cannot give with honesty, it is better to not give at all.

July 2014

"I couldn't t seem to change up my tune about money". I had grown up with a feeling of lack my whole life"....I already sold my gold to keep afloat in 2012.

What a heart breaking day that was. I sold off my gold from my "fella" a Nefertiti pendant, flower, gold chain, bracelet and earrings...as well as every piece of gold that I had so that I could pay the rent. Interesting thing, turns out that Shaworski set of ear rings were nothing more than a set of knock offs given to me in the box!

I would have had more respect had they just left the ear rings in the original packing! Obviously, one could not afford to give the real thing when they lived in a 4 million dollar home and employed a staff of 6.

That showed me where I truly stood in the bigger picture. I was merely a servant. The problem solver whose gratitude price is that of a $3.00 set of ear rings.

Although, it is about doing my job and not about the gifts but for me, it is the principle behind the motive.

That was the "gift" that I was paid as a "friend" after sorting out children suffering from anorexia, absent father issues, bulimia, attention deficit and extended family rebelling against the trials and tribulations of growing up in a restrictive culture.

Who could blame them really? I am no Ghandi, I myself had a past! Who hasn't quite frankly! So, why would teen agers be any different in the east than in the west!

I totally got it! That was them expressing themselves! Their equivalent to throwing another brick in the wall! Sex, drugs and rock and roll! Drink Bacardi and smoke a roll!

A child that had the brains of Einstein with the body of Marilyn Monroe with a tongue that could clip a hedge! I loved her immediately! Another untamed mustang! She bucked when someone tried to tame her!

What could I do when I came upon that lot at the hotel partying over spring break? They had no one to teach them what to do. So that was the day I got the nickname "The Prophet". Knowing how the culture of communities operate and that your "family name" is everything.

I offered the advice, when you cannon ball off the wall into the pool, jump away from the wall. Keep your head forward and protect yourself with your hands. Make sure that you don't piss off the other guests.

It is not only just about you! Don't drink booze and smoke pot together. Don't mix the two. One is a depressant and one is an – anti – depressant. One or the other, not both! No booze in the hot tub!

If you are going to drink in the public eye, put your drink in a go cup or better yet, leave it in your room! Never, ever, and I repeat, ever, drink and drive! Puke in the toilet if you need to, a burger is a sure fire cure for a hangover, drink a load of water with every drink you take and "if you are going to go there", tarp it! No glove, no love! Even better, boys keep the zipper up and girls, keep your legs closed!

What else could I say? The prophet sat in the hot tub for three hours with them teaching the ways of the world. The staff of the Ritz Carlton hotel thanked me. They had been out of control for the last few days. It was spring *break and they were partying like rock stars! Everyone needs to let off a little steam every now and again, even teenagers! "Let's cut "footloose", but do it responsibly!*

What lesson did I learn from that experience? Money does not buy you happiness! I also learned the lengths that one would go to protect the reputation of the family. Even if that meant putting one so called "friend" in a position of being totally compromised legally and professionally!

I would take one visit the hotel that year, and on that day I would find out the answers to questions that I had for the last few years. It broke my heart, but at least, I knew the truth in the end. There again...I loved the kids...I had fun...but what happens to people when they grow up? What happens to their integrity? What happens when money corrupts?

There is nothing more fulfilling for me then sitting in the company of intelligent people having great conversation hanging out by the sea, strumming the guitar, singing some songs and sharing some food and laughs by the fire.

I prefer smaller groups of people. I like to really get to know a person in depth. I keep my social circle small and my inner circle even smaller. My time is precious and I do not put myself into situations that I am not going to enjoy. I live my life with a pure sense of purpose.

As Buddha said, "The mind is everything. What you think you become". I find the greatest peace when I am near water and in nature. The sound of the sea completely calms me, as does the smell of the sea and lake air. It balances out my internal energy sensors. Or my G.P.S – or Gods perfect sensor.

That guide inside of you acts like a global positioning system telling you at any given moment, yes, give me more please or when that feeling doesn't feel so good, it tells you that you are deserving of something better that is your truth.. Everyone has those kinds of feelings...in fact, everyone on the planet has them...

Sometimes this energy in motion that in circulating in our chests is pretty tough to control. The energy overpowers our abilities to express ourselves in words that we release that very negative energy from our mouths...or through our fists.

I think that the best way that I can describe that energy is like a firecracker exploding in your chest. Like little shots of electricity. We might release that overwhelming energy of love and joy through our tears when our cup runs over with the love and adoration that we feel in our hearts in that moment and the tears are released and then fall. I think that everyone can relate to those feelings....

Those feelings that well up inside of your chest when you are overwhelmed with an energy that seems to come out of nowhere...I think that you know the feeling...It's that feeling that one gets when they are experiencing the feeling of awe, or accomplishment, or grief or sorrow, everyone has felt like hell at one time in their life....that feeling of inspiration inside when you are truly overwhelmed by something...that is your truth! That energy can heal and that same energy can destroy!

I love the city, but I love the country life too. To see the beauty of the stars shining so bright. One can't see the magnificence of the night sky in the city. There is a sense of calmness and peace that one does not get from the energy of the city.

Cities for the most part are impersonal with communities really sticking to themselves. It's not like that with rural living. At least not in my little village.

I grew up in a rural community in Manitoba. I come from a huge family and a very long line of teachers. I grew up in a village that had 4 streets and one paved road. My father had 9 brothers and sisters and my mom had 8. We had our own kind of culture.

Every community does. I come from an agricultural region with land as far as the eye can see. Nature was my classroom and everyone owned a hockey stick, a baseball bat and a fishing rod!

I had a very unique upbringing. For the first 5 years of my life, I never really left my village. The only people that I ever saw were the people who lived in my community, my brother, my family and those who came to our family café.

My father and mother owned the local café, my father also drove the school bus and my mother also worked with the elderly.

We were active within our small community. Everyone worked together to bring services that we did not have. The community center was built by volunteers, as was the ball diamond.

I grew up with the expectation that I was to contribute back to my community. I also saw firsthand, the sacrifices that it took and the amount of people it takes to make a community truly operate. It also took a community to raise a child...that was the mentality then...

Life in the 30"s - 50's -80's

"If you fell out of line, your mom and dad knew about it before you got home! If you lipped off the school, you got it twice as hard at home! Everyone in my town was my parent. That is village life and extended family living. There were lines of respect with the elders that you just didn't cross".

It always felt a little off to us as kids to open our mouths and speak disrespectfully to our parents...we just never thought about it because it was never an option"!

"It was the Ukrainians and Polish vs the English. Chain gangs in the streets with the town policeman enforcing laws to have the streets cleared by 9 pm. Township Vs Township, the "jam eaters" vs the "garlic snappers" with fists flying in the hockey rinks. "The Angusville Flyers vs the Rossburn Hornets, Russell Barley Kings, Shoal Lake Eagles, Foxwarren Falcons, or The Angusville Cardinals VS the Birtle Blue Jays and so on.

There was so much competition that our clubs began recruiting the "Yanks" to strengthen baseball clubs to take the game of baseball to the "next level". It was cool to watch. My mom and other ladies in the community used to feed these boys. They would come to our house after the home games to "ice" their arms".

I watched my brother and his friends play football with the "spear chuckers". The losers had to buy the other team a 2L or 6 pack of Coca-Cola and a box of chips! There was amazing community support cheering on our boy's on the ball field or on the ice. Like I said, "every community has its own kind of culture".

We have all evolved and embraced one another removing the labels, but that was the reality for that time. Our region had produced many successful people, NHL hockey players and Gold Medal Olympians as a result of community spirit and competitiveness that was instilled for the love of sport. We play to win, we play hard, we achieve, we shoot and we score!

My brother is a naturally talented guy. He maximized everything that he did when he played sports! I have my brother to thank for instilling that feeling of competition in me. When I was growing up, I wanted to be just like him! I still get a feeling of pride when I remember reading the headlines in the paper "Chuchmuch too much"!

How could I not be proud of that? I helped to create him as he did me. I am his number one fan! We have had a lifetime of ups and downs but one thing that I know with my brother.... It's to the death for us both!

We may hammer one another....but when the chips are down...no matter what...family is family...blood is thicker than water! To the death! I love you, but sometimes, I really just want to punch you right in the face!

We embraced the outdoors growing up. We swam in the local lakes in the summer and skated and played hockey on the pond in winter. I didn't really have much for toys but a Holly Hobby lunch kit and a Big Bird stuffed animal.

My uncle used to joke, he would say we were so poor, mom would cut holes in my pockets so that I had something to play with! We used to play hockey on the kitchen floor with combs and a taped up ball, and used to use the pots, pans and boxes in the house to play musical instruments in our pretend "band". Like the" All Ukrainian Canadian Manitoban" "Partridge Family".

We used to dance together in the kitchen at the farm like the Ingalls's family on the "Little House on the Prairie". My uncles playing the guitar and my grandfather playing the fiddle with everyone singing together.

All of us kids huddled together sleeping in the same bed. We may not have had a lot of money, but we did have love, humor and we were present in one another's lives. We made our own fun. We always seemed to be doing something indoors and outdoors and there was always food and music!

I come from a mother and grandparents who could make "something" from "nothing". They most certainly are the last of the "built to last – repair – re-use – re-build it culture". They managed to live sustainably.

They lived off the land celebrating the bountiful harvest of what nature was able to produce in their backyards. They fed themselves, and they also fed many others. If your buddy was face down on the ground, you picked him up! That is just what you do, no questions asked!

Why did they do that? Simply put, because you knew what it was like to have nothing and it was just the right thing to do!" They grew up in a time of true traditions, had honor and integrity. Your word meant something. "The equivalent to shaking Sinatra's hand".

It's an honor code that was engrained into society. One that is no longer a part of our culture sadly…we are not producing cultures of honor and integrity…we are producing cultures of entitlement, disrespect and blame communities.

Societal thinking has changed so much from that time. What has changed in our societies from then to now? Oscar Wilde said it best, "Nowadays, people know the price of everything and the value of nothing. Albert Einstein feared that technology would raise generations of idiots.

Have you looked at how people are socializing these days? Who is really talking to one another? What do we value as a society? We have bigger houses but smaller families, we have advanced medicine but have poorer health, we have wider freeways but narrower viewpoints, and we have taller buildings but shorter tempers.

As Will Smith said, "we spend money we haven't earned on things that we do not need to impress the people that we don't like". We have embraced the information and technological highway and it has not come without its difficulties.

Isn't it something how technology that brings us close to those that are far away takes us from away from the people whom are actually close to us in physical space?

There are billions of messages sent per day via social media but half of the people say they are lonely. Isn't it ironic that we have more degrees but lese sense, more knowledge but less judgement, more expertise but less solutions, as Martin Luther King said, "We have guided missiles but misguided men".

We have been all the way to the moon and back but we struggle to start a conversation across the street. This is the irony and a paradox of our times and we actually thrive off of this paradox. It is this paradox that actually makes current media interesting.

It's what makes journalism interesting, it's what makes politics interesting and makes television interesting. It is what we feed off and what we live off and what we talk about and discuss.

So how do we bring about a change? How do we dissect this paradox that exists in our lives How do we change the patterns of our culture as we move forward into the 21st century? What cultural behaviors are worth preserving and what culture is worth letting go?

We must self-reflect and ask ourselves, how did I get to this point and time? Is there equal expectation of all people of all cultures in all communities to contribute back to the development of society? What is causing the breakdowns in our societal thinking forward?

Do all societies on the planet accept that it is ok to accept the thought of the "books" of others? That is what these interpretations are, they are books, written by amazing teachers who interpreted energy based on the realities of their environments of the times they were written. Everything else that happens is a result of the systems thinking in the cultural environment.

What is Culture?

So...what is culture and how is culture developed? Culture is what is going on all around you...the way that things are done in your "hood". (Neighborhood).

What is your story? Why do you think the way that you do? What are your team's colors? Who or what do you pay your homage to? What impacts your thought and life experience that makes you decide to make the choices that you do?

The Italians have a wonderful aspect of their culture. It is called Il Dolce Fernente. "The art of doing nothing". This is not only evident in Italy, this is all throughout the European Union.

I love the Europeans for this very real fact. They have mastered this much needed skill! They stop every day and step back, relax, have a glass of red, or have a cup of coffee and just chill out and relax! In the east, you have a cup of Karak, smoke a bit of sheesha, eat some kabab and hang out by the beautiful sea.

In Amsterdam, you get on our peddle bike with your fresh food and ride on home to connect with your family! *"There is nothing better than experiencing a sun rise and set on the canal in the Netherlands or observing a full moon in the heart of the desert.*

There is nothing better than observing the natural wonders of the sky period! There is so much that we do not know about what is beyond us...so much that has yet to be truly discovered...what is truly out there in our universe?

This is an untapped resource that scientists have yet to

truly discover the reality of what "truly is out there". Planets that have been shown to have more intelligent life on them, with more intelligent and societies that are more progressive than ours. Think about the positives of what they can teach us.

I particularly love the sun rise and the sun set. I have observed the sun and the moon all over the globe. I have watched the sun rise and set on the Savanah overlooking Mount Kilimanjaro, while watching the giraffes and lions roam in the distance in Kenya. I have sat on the bench in front of the Taj Mahal in Agra India.

I have watched the sun set on the beaches of Goa, on the Ganges River in Varanasi, at the temples of New Delhi to the beaches of Unawatuna in Sri Lanka, to the shores of the Arabian Gulf, to the rolling hills and mountains of Lebanon.

I have seen the sun set over the amazing blue beaches of the Andaman Sea in Thailand and over the jungles of Surat Thani. I have watched the sun rise on the promenade in Nice, France and set over the sprawling hills of Wales.

I have watched the sun set over Stonehenge in England, while listening to the chimes of Westminster Abbey to watching the sun set over the Loch's in Ireland to the 5 great lakes of Canada, to Old Montreal, Ontario Place to the Rocky Mountains in Alberta and British Columbia.

I have watched the sun rise and set over the strip in Las Vegas to the babbling brook in Virginia to the to the sprawling fields of the prairies in Manitoba and Saskatchewan, from the Atlantic on the East coast to the Pacific on the West to my quiet country village in Angusville".

There are so many things to see, do and experience in the world. The world is an amazing place and I wanted to see everything! I still do! I was inspired by the movie "The Bucket List". Where one makes up a list of all the things that they want to do before they "kick the bucket".

I mostly travel alone by planes, trains, bus, automobile, peddle bike, motor bike, scooter, boat, tuk tuk, elephant, camel, horse and sometimes with an All-Terrain Vehicle, although after an unfortunate ATV accident in Canada in 2010 that would mess me up for a couple of years, I have graduated safer forms of transportation.

Thank goodness my neighbor in my community overseas was the "OT" at the hospital that was treating me. My pal would provide the support that I needed to heal my pelvis and my arm. That sucked. I experienced what it was like to be incapacitated where I could not wipe my own back side!

It was a humiliating and challenging experience at the same time. Do you know what it is like to not have the use of your limbs?

That certainly gave me a new appreciation of those people who live their lives who had it worse than me. I held on to the idea that one day, my "Invictus" would come.

It was during this time, I began reading three books a week and turned this project into global education reform research. I couldn't walk and I couldn't move, so I read, and read, and read some more.

I could have handled that entire situation in one of two ways. Through the eyes of optimism or pessimism. I found the strength to fly back to the Middle East, two weeks after my accident to work with my students to keep the roof over my head and pay the rent.

I would manage to drive myself to my appointment at the hospital, with my casted right arm, tying to shift the manual gears of my car. I would pay a heavy price for many years in my body as a result of that fun.

That year, I bought myself a treadmill and worked on gaining the strength in my body to walk. I went to my last business meeting that year in October. I put on a brave face, but I was so full of pain killers.

I would only meet with one person that year to discuss education. I had to heal myself. But...live and learn...I turned the very negative situation into a positive and kept on, keeping on!

My magic carpet has been to a lot of places! The more that I know, is the more that I don't know and the more that I want to experience and find out." Most every country that I have visited, I try to visit an airport, hospital, school, and orphanage and experience the "religion" and culture practiced in the environment.

*I typically travel alone as it forces me to get out of my comfort zone and talk to strangers and meet local people. I eat at local restaurants and hire a local guide to show me the non-commercialized "sites" or just get out there on my own and explore on foot or motor bike. When in Rome, do as the locals do, but **"Act local, think global"**.*

"The situations that I have managed to find myself in over the years while traveling has been something. I visited India 6 times. Each time for a different purpose from healing holidays to studying Vedic astrology and Ayurveda. This country is purely an assault on one's senses. There is no way to describe the experience of India. It is a planet by itself.

Everything that you see, taste, smell, touch and hear in this culture is unlike anything that you have ever experienced before. It is amazing how this country manages to operate with the size of population.

There is extreme culture in every society however, in India, it is quite something to see the differences from the poor to the wealthy and on the same street. Slumdog millionaire is right!

What diversity of culture in the borders of one country! I do not understand the reasoning and the mentality of some cultural food choices.

When there is hungry people on the streets and cows roaming free that would provide so much food for the people who are starving. Put the cows to pasture, milk them and eat them! Your people are hungry!

Why is this logic so hard to embrace in the 21st century? I do not understand this thinking and the reasoning behind it.

I began my love affair with the Netherlands culture in 2002. I believe all that I could say was "holy shit"! Are you serious the first time I arrived!

This is freedom unlike what I had ever seen before! I have tried to study every aspect of the thought in this culture and why the people think the way that they do.

Specifically, cannabis culture. Can I really walk into a café and order off the menu, have a cup of coffee, read the paper and have it not be illegal?" What planet am I on?

There are cures for Cancer that the world does not know about? They filed patents for how many different kinds of strains? WHAT??? Are you "shitting" me? "Chouish", are you serious? Walla?? NO....It can't be true?

They would never dream of withholding the cure for cancer? Who would do that? Why would someone with hold natural cures? Could it be for money?

I have serious questions about this *"New World Order"*. How can countries not have the same free movement as everyone else on the planet? I do not understand this logic that every person on the planet does not have equal access to a countries borders or that one country passport has more "weight" than others.

Why are some nationalities allowed to enter and others not? Why do we still have people on this planet that do not have a registered passport so that the people can state "this is my homeland"?

The people in the country did not make the mistakes of the "leadership" running it and yet, the common man, faces the consequences of the leadership at the top.

There is no denying that law and order is required for

the functioning of our societies. Where would we be without the wonderful governmental leaders who have inspired us forward as human beings? Our world functions because of leaders. What happens however, when money corrupts?

The "fat cats", make their decisions understanding that it will never impact them as these types of leadership that are operating the world operate above us all and never have to wait in the "bread" line.

They don't really care about the impact of the decision because frankly, they have never once been in the position to feel, what if it was me?

These people are entering countries on their private planes never having to really go through "border control". They aren't the ones that have families blown up in the market place when they go out to buy the basic necessities that a family needs to live.

But… it is only the common man, what does it matter? Human rights and dignity do not matter! I guess that must be a "class" thing. Perhaps it's designed that way? That is a whole lot of power to have. Who would want to spread that freedom of movement lifestyle around?

It gives those that have lived their entire lives in the cheap seats something to work toward and achieve! It gives us something to talk about!

People in the developed nations have no idea what poverty means. Traveling though India, Thailand, Africa and Sri Lanka where people are sleeping in a hammock in the trees or begging for food in the streets. I cannot understand these nations and how whole societies of people are living in such squalor in the 21st century?

How can we live in such an extreme world where parts of the globe can have so much and some parts can have so little? Where is the logic? Who is profiting, because it certainly isn't the common people?

Now, in 2017, having put the puzzle pieces together understanding the systems thinking of how our world truly operates, my perspective of "democracy" has completely changed as I realized a far greater iron fisted tyranny existed within the systems thinking of those that were spreading their "riotousness" exploiting economies and people for their resources as opposed to supporting with formations of true democratic societies.

"Everything is a rich man's trick, from the "Middle East Project", to the Hitler project to JFK to 911! What is the point of wars? As Sam Giancana, said, "War is just a money racket, people give their lives so that a few "fat cats" can make a killing"!

But who are those fat cats? Who benefits most from the sales of arms, guns and "weapons of mass destruction"? Who benefitted most from the holocaust? Do we really think that one man had the power to create so much destruction on his own? Hitler had quite a lot of help! Our world has not been given the "truth" as to who and what is really holding the gun.

Author Oliver Stone wrote it best, "Treason doth never prosper,' wrote an English poet, 'What's the reason? For if it prosper, none dare call it treason.

War! What is it good for? Who benefits?

Many people have perished in the 20th century because there is a lack of accountability with the 'fat cats". It is time for the people to take back their power! The 21st

century has had quite enough of industrialized thought energy that has been controlling the hand of "God" that controls our rights to freedom of movement and the evolution of our societal thinking forward!

People in the west are lead to believe that destruction through war is warranted. This is done through misuse of the media spreading "Islamophobia", fear and through "false flag" operations **giving a reason to the public to justify the money spent on "war"**!

War and oil are big businesses, could the two be related? Could there truly be other ways of harnessing energy without so much death and destruction?

Scientists as far back as the time of Nicola Tesla in the 1930"s have been stifled by the establishment because their advancements forward toward free energy development is far more cost effective.

May 2016

"Everyone has their breaking point and I reached mine on the 22 of May in 2016. No amount of money would make me compromise my integrity and my values as an educator. I don't care what title you may carry, that is

your child, and I am the teacher! Your child is your responsibility to raise, not mine!

I am not a bad teacher! I will not say that it is ok for your son to turn in his work done by the Science tutor and I will not say that it is ok for your son to cheat on his English paper.

For the third time, it is not the schools fault, it is your son's fault, the tutors fault and lastly, it is your fault for not following up as a parent! It is not my responsibility to be responsible for your son when he is in your care nor is it my responsibility to discipline him when he is at school or at home with you!

I am not a terrible teacher, you are a terrible parent! I knew at that moment...it was time to go! The messenger yet again was being shot and the price that I was paying was far too high as a human being to educate other's children. No way was I going to eat that "shit sandwich"!

Being that loose lipped, I knew, it was not going to be long before I was like "Wiley Coyote" on the acme rocket and would find my backside with a one way ticket *out of the country or in jail!*

The hypocrisy of that whole situation and what transpired at that final parent meeting was too much for me to handle. Having to endure the inadvertent throwing of "I am in total power and control in my face was a little much". Even when she decided to send over the plate of food to the maid sitting with the children while the Egyptian ladies had their breakfast at the next table.

I was living from my hand to my mouth because I could not afford the rent. For the last 5 months she was late with my pay. Weather that was deliberate? I had nothing left to continue for in the East. It was then that I realized, why am I here? I deserve better!

I don't deserve any more treatment like this and I couldn't handle another kick from another national that was above the law! How many times had I fixed their children and then was kicked for doing it!

ENOUGH! I AM EXAUSTED! That was the tipping point. I was struggling to remember the feeling of the positive of why I came in the first place. It was time to go. I woke up on too many mornings in that last year looking at myself in the mirror saying is this it for me?

Why am I here? "Is this as good as it is going to get"? I was growing weaker and weaker....I could not stand on my own two feet anymore....it was getting harder and harder to re-charge my batteries and to find the "positive" in my current situation.

"Prime Minister Trudeau's positive energy "lit me up" like a lighthouse and beckoned me home as after living in the "old world" for 15 years in the east, where free speech and free thought were not observed "I was dying a slow death inside! I had forgotten what it felt like to "feel free"!

I had forgotten how to use my voice to speak. There had been so many ups and downs over the years. I had many successes, but I also had many failures. I couldn't take the roller coaster ride and the instability any more so, I sold off everything I owned and a month later, moved back to Canada" to replenish and start again. I went back to my roots where I could legally speak.

Leaders have the ability to inflict great powers of

positive or negative energy into environments creating cultures of innovation, diversity and acceptance in to their environments or breed cultures of fear, hate, racism, control and contempt.

Canada's Prime Minister the Right Honorable Justin Trudeau inspired the globe with his positive energy celebrating cultural diversity embracing differences as a strength changing the "tune of the frequency of the energy" of Canada in a very short time from negative to positive.

As Prime Minister Trudeau said, "We've gotten an important thing right in Canada. Not perfect, but right. That thing is the balance between individual freedom and collective identity. We know that people are defined in large part by our relationships to other people. Our cultural background, our gender, our religious beliefs, our sexual orientation. However, we also believe that all of those collective associations receive their highest expression in the form of real, flesh and blood, individual human beings. We expand cultural freedom by ensuring that individual Canadians who come from these diverse communities have the freedom to live and express and grow and change their cultures. We refuse to see a contradiction between individual liberty and collective identity. In fact, we have created a society where both thrive, and mutually reinforce one another. It was at its root, a leap of faith, and a very new idea. Over time, we learned to trust that whatever their culture of origin, the more people engage with the breadth of our country's diversity, the more Canadian they will become. Where there was repression, it would be defeated by the more compelling Canadian opportunity to achieve liberty. Where there was isolation, we would meet it with openness and inclusion. It may have started as a leap of faith, but it has become a defining characteristic of our country, our great success, and arguably our greatest contribution to the world. We have proven that a country—an astonishingly successful country—can be built on the principle of mutual respect".

"The 2016 election of Donald Trump as president of the United States has stunned the world and raised a number of extremely critically important issues about the future of United States government policy and the impact on a global scale. Among these are aspects of national security law, including the extent of government surveillance and secrecy, the use of drones for targeted killings, the detention and interrogation of suspected terrorists, immigration and refugee policies, and the deployment of U.S. forces in various roles across the Middle East". Foreign Affairs Magazine 2017

Former American President, John Fitzgerald Kennedy, deemed by history as one of the greatest leaders of democracy inspired the world with his words in his inaugural address leaving us a road map for non-violent peaceful solutions.

The world is not different diplomatically from when his words were spoken in 1961, as now more than ever, our rights and freedoms as free citizens of the world are under threat.

The United States foreign policy impacts systems thinking and policy and procedure around the globe. As the world waits in anticipation wondering what will happen, we have taken a more progressive approach! For those of us that understand the law of attraction and the impact of energy, we could see it coming! **We were right on the money**!

March 2017

"I may not agree with the politics of the leadership in the east, however, to have their economies toppled for access to their oil is a little much for any person to comprehend. Why is the world freaking out over whose

book is right and whose society is better than the other? With that being said, to the east..."it is not your book that frightens the people in the west, it is components of your culture".

As an educator and one who loves God as much as the next person, why do I have to be a Muslim to visit the shrine of your most beloved leader? I wanted to visit but you wouldn't let me! You said it yourselves, "I am an infidel"! Your words...not mine!

Same thought applies to the Buddhists, Hindu's and every other religious shrine that I have wanted to enter but couldn't because I chose to find my way to god through another book. I wanted to pay my respects but I could only get to the door to knock. You would not open it to let me in!

If I have to fit into your culture when I am living in your borders....ok...by that estimation...you must adhere to the culture in my community...and that means...your book of enlightenment...must remain in your backpack in public education and in the public forum.

In the west, we promote multiple intelligence education

and that includes expression of one's self through questioning and learning from "all books".

Let us all gather together in prayer and meditation showing gratitude for being alive! THANK YOU...THANK YOU....Let's have a happy day! We are a united global community! We all just want to be happy, healthy thriving and living in peace. Let us bring back the arts in our schools so that we can develop new cultural expression.

I may not agree with how "President Trump conveyed his message while wearing a gold cross on his neck, he sailed the titanic completely through democracy and shot a hole right through lady liberty, in his effort to convey a message being the voice of almost half of the American people who felt that they were not being heard.

The people spoke their truth through the vote! But did they? Is it a true democracy when the popular vote of the country is not counted? Hmm...the vote. A right in which we take for granted. A right that many people on this planet do not yet have.

Most people spend their times in front of their television, assuming that what media is being fed to them is accurate and correct. Much of that culture filters down into your homes and into your thoughts and then into your actions.

I agree with Mr. Trump...take care of your own first and then you can take care of other, but please be the leader all of your people can be proud of.

And seriously...We "Snow Mexicans" north of the USA border are thinking....didn't we already witness the falling of the Berlin wall? I don't know...something to think about I guess...History does repeat.

Although, can you see Russia from your house too"? I am happy that America will take care of home first. A question for all leadership. Is it truly noble to kill for your cause? Why is war an option? When will our world experience peace? Where are the peace talks?

Think, speak and feel solutions! Think positive! Think, how can I help? What do you need? Extend your hand in support and demonstrate gratitude. Every culture has its own problem's. Denial is not a river in Egypt!

To solve the problem we have to admit that there is one and face it head on! It will hurt, but it's better to know...then not know... Leaders inspire negative or positive change cultures! That is truth!

All systems thinking is not perfect...everything is a work in progress...everything needs a tune up every now and again...that is what creates progress....when you know what you don't want...it brings you closer to knowing what you do want.....We can always stop....and change our thought....reframe and start again....the cycle continues.

The thing is...do you really know what it is that you want? How do you know? Think...how did that thought make me feel? What you focus your attention on, you will get more of. Where your attention goes, energy flows and experience grows through the law of attraction.

Now knowing this information, the quality of my thoughts are something like...

"I am so excited for the future. I figured it out for myself. For those that have fallen away because our visions *were no longer a match, let negative do us part... thank you for the experience, both positive and negative. The experience made me who I am today! I embrace my mistakes. I share them and I go back and try it again. Everything is a process in learning.*

There are two sides to every coin and opposites of any equation. It takes two people to contribute to the success or failure of any relationship. I am neither entirely innocent, nor am I guilty but I can take responsibility for the thoughts I think and how act and how I react in the future.

Life goes on and so must I. I hope that we will be on the same "wavelength" again, however, until such time, I will accept, that at this particular time in our lives, we are singing different tunes and are operating at a different wavelength and frequency! I sincerely hope our positive paths will cross again. I wish you all the success on your journey!

Embrace your negative! Source energy will send an electric spark charge through your system that will tell you to take note! Based on the intensity of that charge, you will react. Your body is a battery and a magnet, re-charge it when needed and take a rest! Tune the frequency of your body into joy to experience a lifetime of joy!

As Eleanor Roosevelt said, "No one can make you feel inferior without your consent". Take the time out and really truly think about the quality of your life and the cultures that you are creating in your environments.

Appreciate what you have for when you truly appreciate and are grateful for what you have, more will come. This is what Oprah Wlinfrey has been going on about for years! Look at how she has inspired the world with her thought and her leadership! She had a goal and she went for it!

People who do not have goals work for those who do! Your success of failure is entirely up to you! Your own worst enemy is in between your own two ears!

What's going on in the science of your mind? How are you feeling today? Where are you operating on the emotion tone scale? Are you operating around grief or are you operating at a frequency of joy?

What tunes are you listening to? What songs are playing

out in between your own two ears and what is the tone of the emotional notes of your internal play list? How are your thoughts feeling? If that thought does not feel good, release it!

Talk about it and expel the negative. Talk to your partner, talk to your minister, talk to your doctor, talk to someone. You will find your relief when you expel what is toxic and focus on what is positive!

Negative energy = stop = change the thought, but don't keep on talking about it or thinking about, or feeling about it, because that is what you will get more of!

Never make the biggest decisions in your life with the same feeling of the mind set in which you created the problem! Seek solutions first…tune into the positive…then act!

 One day you will look back and realize that you worried too much about things that don't really matter and you will actually be glad things didn't work out the way you once wanted them to for that meant something better was coming.

Everyone is the same everywhere on the planet. There

are only good and bad choices. All people are inherently good! All people are positive energy! It's time for change…the worlds kids are crying…it is time for them to know the meaning of their tears.

In any environment, when you scratch below the surface, there is always a deeper level of truth based on the influence of the culture of the experiences in the environment.

January 2017

"In the end with this chapter of the opus of my life, I will say, THANK YOU FOR THE EXPERIENCE! I AM SOOOOOOO BLESSED AND GRATEFUL to have had the opportunity to ride Aladdin's magic carpet! We shall meet again for a cup of Karak, Inshallah! ☺

To the little children in the east. Thank you for making my heart sing. If I do not see you again, I shall remember you fondly. In my heart, I didn't give birth to you…but I loved you like I did, otherwise, I would have never "tuned you up".

Thank you for your hospitality and your business! Thank you for reminding me to take care about my family and my community first. ☺ I am blessed to have had the opportunity to experience life in your borders. It has forever changed me for I found solutions to questions I had been asking my entire life.

I found Allah for myself and I wrote a new book about it. What began as a negative, has been turned into a positive learning experience to benefit all. I found my soul's purpose for life.

My purpose for my life is free thought through finding joy. The basis of my life is true freedom. The result of my life is to expand what I have created as a result of the thoughts that I think! Embrace the contrast and mistakes of life for it means, something better is coming"!

Changing your thoughts from negative to positive changes the course of your entire life! Make the choice to become consciously aware of the thoughts that you think!

I AM are two of the most important words in any language for what you put after them, you will most certainly become!

Have fun! Raise your glass and celebrate the opus of your life! Be grateful for the life that you have. For being truly appreciative and grateful for your current life experience, more will come. You mission is to find your joy in everything that you do!

So what inspires me forward? Where is that powerful energy coming from?

December 16, 2011

"I got that dreaded phone call on the 16th of December, 2011. A call that I hoped that I would never get when I was living overseas. That day I had been gardening. I was listening to the song "If today was your last day by Nickelback".

I had never heard the song before. I must have listened to it 200 times that day. The general gist of the song is what would you do if today was your last day? How would you want history to remember you?

When I had come in from my day in the garden there was a message from my brother on the answering machine. My father had made his transition. While I was listening to that song, he was taking his journey. I now know, that was his way of connecting with me and preparing me for what was to come.

What my father could not teach me in life, he taught me in physical death. He taught me what happens when a guy "cashes in his chips". I had always wanted to know. The question - What is truth? The answer - I AM Energy of Mind and Emotion squared! E=ME2

I AM ENERGY and so is my Dad. He is "lighting me up" as we speak...and you too! He left us in physical body, but his energy continues to be all around us.

As is everyone who has gone before is! When one door closes, and so another window to the universe opens! There is no death, only positive constant evolution of life!

Do not fear death as death is transitioning from one plane to another. Now, you travel without the luggage or the clothing or culture of the vessel of the body you chose.

Like all things on the planet, you are energy! Choose your next adventure! YOU ARE TRUTH! Give yourself a tune up and tune into joy!

"Now, it is 2017 and I can now legally speak...I found my voice! Free at last, free at last, thank "God" all mighty I AM free at last! AND....so are my thoughts...I no longer live in fear and I no longer fear people.

What a wonderful thought it is that some of the best days of our lives haven't happened yet! Now that is what I know for sure! Tune into joy and have fun! You are unfinished and unwritten! **Peace! "Chuch is out"!**

Chapter 2 the Problem

I Education Re-design Industrialized Education Models

To move forward with re-designing education systems we must find the balance bridging education past, present and future. We must begin again at "ground zero"! In order to create solutions however, we must examine the past to ensure that history does not repeat in the future.

The current model of education practiced by every country in the world was designed for **industrialized societies in the 19th century teaching students,** "what to think", rather than, "how to think".

The standards movement in education has created a living and breathing academic elitist caste system in assessment models defining all children for life as academic / non-academic / successful / not successful based on ability to achieve 100% on a pencil and paper test score.

In any system of education, the common question that remains at the forefront of everyone's mind is how do we prepare students who are entering into educations systems in present day for life success up until retirement and beyond? As societies continue to evolve, we must prepare students to embrace cultural diversity, modernization and globalization, while seeking knowledge.

What are the issues that people face in our current societies as adults? Sickness, divorce, emotional breakdown, depression, suicide, bullying, anxiety, cancer, and the list goes on.

With the influence of capitalism, medical science has become about treating the disease for money and not the person organically, putting a band aid on the problem as opposed to getting to the root causes and solving the problem for good.

People are having to take medication to combat the medication that they are taking. If we educated children about natural ways to maximize their brains capabilities, preventative health, meditation, and what their emotions meant from a young age, we could alleviate these issues in adults.

What's fun about education these days? Who wants to carry around a ton of books in your back pack? That thought of the past is really heavy to carry around all the time. It is like the equivalent of trying to drive a car forward while looking in the rear view mirror.

Technology lightens the load bringing thought into the 21st century. A million books in my pocket and they don't hold the weight of the world on my back! Kids' today want to travel light! Technology stimulates all the senses.

Technology brings the world to students when they cannot physically experience the world. It is a magic carpet ride in the palm of your hand. What teacher can really compete with that?

So rather than go against the flow of energy that the kids are putting out there, let's embrace it. With that in mind however, a whole entire other set of issues have arisen because of technology.

We have a whole society of kids who do not understand systems thinking of processes, can't sign their name, add and subtract or think for themselves. These days you would be hard pressed to find children playing and exploring outdoors creating their own fun. All these rules and regulations that have taken the fun out of learning through exploratory play and outdoor education.

We have kids as young as one knowing how to power up an iPhone. Kids today are born into a completely different frequency of energy. They are already one hundred miles ahead of you in thought form when you first came to the planet and started your journey.

We hold them back because of our fear of change. We resist the current of their energy until finally, we see that we have no choice but to throw up our hands, change our tune about things and go with the energy flow as this is what they want. Why fight it, embrace it! Some birds are not meant to be caged.

"I AM Hidalgo, the untamed mustang. If things don't feel good inside, I BUCK! Ask my parents about their experiences of trying to control me as a kid.

I banged my head against the couch whenever I was upset or crying, 2 couches later, I think I finally sorted that energy out, only to be greeted with the barrage of the trauma of going to school from my village to the next community.

I wish that I understood the meaning of the energy of my anger and tears. We would see a lot of problems solved in society if we taught people the meaning of their internal energy and their tears. They are there for a reason.

This is the powerful energy that fixes you. When you get tired of feeling the way that you do, by finding the solution to your problem, you will change your frequency of energy in your body. Your anger will be released and the feeling will stop.

Your energy sensors will balance out and resonate at the same frequency that you have trained your body to operate. I would have saved myself a lot of heartache had I known what my emotional guidance system was for. It was meant to tell me, stop, take note and remember".

Students are being stressed out by the negative "grading" structure of the current assessment model. Is the purpose of education systems to develop a world full of professors? Our children's mental health is more important than grades, is it not?

Who wins in this current system of education? What is the definition of life success and who sets that standard? Is life success living in a state of optimal health or is life success getting 100% on a test in reading in writing?

Current systems define children within a set of parameters, telling them, it's ok to be you, as long as it's ok with me! *"I define myself thank you"*! *"Isn't that what you wanted me to do in education in the first place"*?

If we want our students to take responsibility of themselves and of their learning, shouldn't we let them do it? **We are forcing our students to be square pegs fitting into round holes to excel in a system that it just isn't working for all children.**

"I started school in 1976 in a school that had 2 classrooms with 4 grades in each room with 25 students in a classroom per teacher. I can remember all of us together, watching man land on the moon on the black and white television. I was totally in awe and wonder!

OMG!!! Man could walk on the moon! Holy crap! What kind of world was I living in? How cool was that? That same year, I remember finding an old newspaper of Kennedy's assassination under the carpet of my uncles and aunts house thinking to myself what has this man done that was so bad that people would want to hurt him? JFK's energy continues to inspire me today,

At age 6, I spent grade one holding a picket sign in my hands that read "MY TEACHER KNOWS WHO I AM" exercising my right to "free speech" picketing the school division to not close my community school. Our school closed, I spent grade one going to school in a hockey rink. I remember 2 lessons from that year.

I think it is pretty safe to say I entered into the next community school in grade 2 almost illiterate. As was standard practise in education those days, I was immediately ability grouped and labelled as "weak" and "slow". What I wouldn't have given to be with the roadrunners!

Fast forward 30 years or so later. Attending Harvard was something that was always on my "bucket list". In May of 2012, a very dear friend and I went to Harvard

Graduate School of Education in the U.S.A to attend the Think Tank on Global Education conference.

60 countries gathered to discuss Global Education. What an amazing experience that was for us as educators. For me, it was one of the most rewarding experiences of my life.

As I self-reflected in my journal I remembered the feeling, it took me right back to the experience..."I giggled like a school girl when I arrived at the Harvard Gate.

I took a journey of inspiration along the way. I paid my respects to JFK and RFK at Arlington cemetery, I cried tears of joy when I heard Martin Luther King's I have a dream speech over the loud speaker and I attended an Abraham-Hicks workshop in Washington D.C.

Perhaps I took that journey of inspiration to remind myself, I have a voice, I matter and I belong here! I was an egg head that couldn't spell. I hadn't failed...the system had failed me. Some 30 years later, I finally let that feeling of unworthiness go!

It reaffirmed that I was meant to push on with my

research on education reform. The problems that we face as educators are global issues. Children are children everywhere on the planet. A paradigm shift in education is required.

"In the rank of importance in the hierarchy of subjects taught in today's schools. At the top, with the most important emphasis in terms of time spent on development, is language and math, then there are the sciences and humanities in the middle, then vocational subjects and sport and at the bottom are the arts, why don't we treat these subjects equally"? Sir Ken Robinson

Dr. Howard Gardener's theory of multiple intelligence's demonstrates that human beings are capable of expressing themselves through means other than reading and writing.

There are 8 different forms of intelligence found in every human being. Utilizing the child friendly descriptors, we are music, body, people, word, logic, nature, self and picture.

It is not a question of are you smart, rather how are you

smart. The key to excelling and understanding each of these specific areas in the human experience is through repeated exposure through gaining life experience to apply knowledge.

The world is a great tapestry of differentiated and integrated thought. Unfortunately, due to the standards movement being linked to capitalism and competition in logical and mathematical reasoning, success is being defined as reading and writing really well and having a lot of money.

Having a high standard is not a bad thing, we should all have a model to emulate however, what about the artists, musicians, naturalists, dancers and every other human that chooses to express themselves through a mode other than reading and writing?

21st century societies are producing cultures of blame, children are having children and the education sector must compensate for lack of value education that was originally taught at home.

Educators are stretched to the limits with societal expectations of solving the problems of every child, with limited resources as every child has different strengths and needs.

Education is not personalized, rather the model of delivery is designed for mass production with limited resources and limited funding. Educators are expected to solve the problems of society, however, society is making the jobs of educators difficult as the roles of educators change to pick up the "slack" for the rest of societies short comings!

The greed model of businesses operating school boards with wanting "more", for less has taken its toll, on everyone! Systems reform requires cross the board commitment.

"A system of education is only as good as its teachers". UNESCO. Everyone who comes into contact with children is classified as a teacher. It is our station as adults to model cultures of responsibility for youth. Todays' children are tomorrow's leaders, the little people are our future. They see everything that you do!

"A big thought out to the parents, a teacher knows what child is talked at or talked with, a teacher knows what

parent spends time with their children and which parents sit their kids in front of a television. A teacher knows what child is misbehaving because of lack of boundaries that were not enforced at home.

Bullying that is rampant in our schools is because of parents that have zero clue how to manage their own stress, emotions, minds and relationships. The innocence of children is a wonderful thing.

I love everything about education and the possibilities that education provides. I am happiest when I am learning something new each and every day! In fact, I thrive on it! But, everything that I had learned in school, for the most part prepared me for my profession, school did not prepare me for the trials and tribulations of life!

Professional Self- Reflection – How do I learn best as a person? How do I know what I know? What are my strengths? What are my weaknesses and why do I have them? How can I apply this knowledge to my teaching situation? How can I help my students understand the learning process knowing this knowledge about myself and how I learn best? Self-reflect applied to life experience based on the world today. State something positive!

I required quite a lot of repetition for things to become solid in my mind because I didn't have a huge vocabulary of words. Thank God that I did find that one teacher, who for me did "chew her cabbage twice".

That teacher not only taught me how to read and write, she also taught me how to be a great teacher! I have her to thank for shaping my thought as an educator and how to truly manage your class to maximize student achievement. She was the first one to step up to help me financially in this work.

A shout out to those teachers who taught me with manipulatives, with colour, visuals, audio, where I could use my hands to apply what I know. Those lessons I remember.

I remember running the cafeteria, I remember the high school drama, sports, music, choir, creating the yearbook, job shadowing in my community, group projects, community outings, student council, building the bird houses in my shop class, taking apart the small engine in metals, sewing the dress, cooking the food, all the classes that let me move around to think and be creative but unfortunately, we spent so little time learning in today's schools but desperately need.

I guess that explains why if you walked into one of my classes, more often than not, you wouldn't find my students sitting at a table. I could care less where they sat, if they stood, laid on the floor, in a tent, under a desk, on a ball, or a t-stool, or standing desk, sat in a wheel chair, standing frame, or expressed themselves though word, music, video or paint, or needed to communicate using sign language because they could not hear, or pictures to communicate if they could not speak.

If that is what the student needed to help them learn and process information to express what they knew at their level of understanding, I let them go for it! Whatever floats your boat!

Win win...they get their work done and I get my objective completed. Those children who could not speak were my greatest teachers. I had to learn how to communicate using other senses as did they. "Silence is my language, can you hear it"? Allchin There are more ways to communicate and express one's self other than through oral language and the written word!

I don't remember a whole lot from all of my lessons, but I do remember the way that I felt when I was in them. Although, I experienced a great deal of struggle within the structure of the current model of education it is because of this struggle however, that I understand the process of learning and knowledge application. THANK YOU CONTRAST! It is how we learn.

It took a community to raise this child and as a result of the values instilled in me by my family, community and country, I was taught from a very young age to speak out for injustice and the importance of community development. I was also taught the value of work and what it means to have to contribute to achieve.

Today's kids, I am not sure that they understand that concept. So what has changed within our societies? Have we done our kids a service or a dis service to them by making their lives easier so that they don't have to struggle like we did?

"My parents taught me the value of work by working in our family café serving the people at age 5. This is where I learned math. Hands on learning! I had an allowance of 2 bucks a week! As I got older, that incentive grew to $5, then $10, then $20.

I started formal employment when I was 12 years old. I remember how great it felt to run home with my first pay check in hand. Wa hooo...just like Fred Flintstone sliding off the dinosaur when the shift came to a close! Score Chuchmuch!

For my 16th birthday I was given the gift of learning how to change the oil in the family car and how to change the tire in case I got a flat.

30 jobs later, from being a baker, waitress, shop attendant, babysitter, coach, labourer, farm hand, construction worker, laundry service worker, as I grew, so did the requirement for hands on knowledge that was required for each life and societal process. Clearly, I learn on the job"!

These days education is not an exactly an easy profession to be in. Everyone points the finger at you the educator to take responsibility for something that ultimately educators cannot change. Educators are working with a system that has become obsolete with a world full of people who expect the school to solve all of their problems with child rearing at home.

Is it our job to parent children or educate them? There is a huge difference! My question to society, what's wrong with a little struggle? Not that I expect kids to be raised in concentration camps but how will children ever know and appreciate success if they do not know the feeling of failure?

Making mistakes is how people learn. I can't tell you how many mistakes I have made in my lifetime. I look forward to making a few more!

"Brains run the world. They run the stock market and the local market. They run huge corporations and the mom and pop shop down the street. Brains run churches, banks, hotels, clubs, sports teams, the internet and universities.

Brains run marriages, choirs, homeowners associations and terrorist groups. Your brain runs you and is involved in running your family, yet even though the brain is involved with everything we do at work and at home, we rarely think about or honour the brain.

There is no formal education about the brain in MBA programs, no brain-training programs at church, no brain exercises in customer service or management programs and no real practical education about the brain in school. The lack of brain education in schools is a huge mistake" Dr. Daniel G. Amen.

Those that have made the greatest impact on humanity attest their success to thinking differently. Steve Jobs described these people as the "crazy ones, the misfits, the rebels, the round pegs in the square holes, the ones who see things differently.

They are not fond of rules and they have no respect for the status quo. You can quote them, disagree with them, glorify or vilify them, about the only thing that you can't do is ignore them, because they change things, they push the human race forward.

And while some may see them as being the crazy ones, we see genius, because the people who are crazy enough to change the world, are the ones who do".

Look at what he did to contribute to society.

He followed his intuition, changed his thinking and he inspired many. He continues to live on today in all of us and our technology. He left a great legacy for us, as did many others!

What do you value? Where do your values come from? Being grateful and appreciative of the life that one has brings more positive things to one's life. Being ungrateful brings more negative things….Choose your thoughts and actions wisely.

Are you appreciative in nature or are you taking things for granted? Respect and values aren't taught through an "app". We can't rely on Apple, Google, Samsung, Blackberry, Facebook, YouTube or Microsoft for the solutions for that one. There must be a balance.

Have you remembered to say thank you? Do you express your appreciation and gratitude? Are you truly present in your life and in the lives of your children, spouse or otherwise? Do they have to book an appointment to spend time with you?

Remember, "The apple" does not fall far from the tree

in the "Garden of Eden". The little people that come forth from you are your responsibility to raise. They are you after all! Your energy inspires them to come forward. Your "mini ME's are your responsibility! Everyone has a job to do when it comes to education reform.

With the influx of immigration, modernization and globalization, societies are expressing growing concerns for preservation of national identity and culture. In order to preserve culture, we must teach culture.

All nations face issues of preservation of national identity as a result of "cultural" influence. The question remains, what culture is worth preserving as we move forward into the 21st century?

Culture is a broad subject and includes not only expression of self though music, art and dance and the like, culture is also the practice of environments. Influence of the media, pop culture, capitalism, governmental structures, family and community thought formulate culture and all have a direct influence over the mind and the formation of values practiced by each individual.

One level of society and culture impacts another. Our systems thinking has caused great discord in many levels of society and the school cannot solve all of the problems in society.

Educators are educators and they are not parents. Everyone must take responsibility for their roles in society. Teachers can no longer be everything to everyone. Everyone needs to take responsibility for their part in creating cultures of responsibility.

Chapter 3
Policy Analysis Culture Impacting Thought East / West

Through observation of the Eastern adult population, visiting governmental, education, medical, private and non-profit sector departments, living as a resident within the population, engaging in business activities, working with the adult population, these same tendencies were present within systems thinking and processes in every organization where "privileged" nationals had been given excessive governmental support were employed.

Although, it would not be correct to assume blanket judgement on all nationals, however, as stated, these tendencies were highly prevalent within systems thinking within the culture.

The population demonstrated a lack of intrinsic motivation to learn and accept responsibility, more specifically, members of the ruling elite, have been raised with the understanding that they will never ever have to work to earn financial capital as it will be given to them because of their "privileged status". The value of work is not promoted, rather, the idea that "money" will solve the problems by someone else is promoted.

Society passes judgement on "labour" related jobs being for people of a lower "class" and are classified as being roles for "the help" with children being raised to believe that these tasks are "beneath" them, all the while, all children are being raised by the paid "help".

*Note**Free speech is not permitted, negative media or negative feedback about the crown is not tolerated. It is culturally insulting to point out faults though direct communication. "High context", indirect communication is the common practise thus making the creation of cultures of responsibility extremely difficult as "trust" is not based on word, rather based on "family reputation".

Group societies alleviate the need for individuals to accept "responsibility", with one often internalizing thought of the group to remain a part of that constant unit. One would not risk being different as this impacts the entire family unit as a whole, which impacts how well the family will function within the tribal unit within the structure of the society.

All people do not openly voice negative emotion or typically openly express discontent with any person in the community. Most negative is internalized and readily accepted as no choice because of the reality of the environment with laws being fluid and negative behaviour not openly addressed because what happens with one person, impacts the whole unit.

Shia vs Sunni religious views are still very prevalent within the systems thinking in the children. Children are being raised to hate not understanding the reasons why.

Specifically geared toward the Shia population. Strict societal codes of conduct with male and female interacting continues to dominate. Children are rebelling, wanting to embrace outside thought and freedoms, however, the "energy gap", and what is tolerated in the religious "book" and what is "cultural acceptable" is causing great discord within the generational thought process and societal cultural expectations.

Strong moral values and expectations are placed within the communities with both women and men believing that their bodies are sacred and should only be revealed to the eyes of the one that they love.

Traditional courting of male and female continues with supervised visitations among the sexes. Inter-family marriages also continue to dominate with parents arranging the spouse of the woman or man.

One does not marry for love, rather one marries to ensure the safety of the family resources and continue the family line of resources to ensure survival of the family and community.

Marriages are viewed very pragmatically, more like a business arrangements formulated without emotion. Through time, love evolves through respect gained by facing the trials and tribulations of life. Some relationships are healthy, others, extremely un-healthy.

Divorce rates are continually on the rise in all societies, with all cultures experiencing discord in relationships with severing relational ties and assumption of responsibilities for child rearing.

Western cultures have experienced a breakdown in family values. In the efforts to achieve equality as women they have become men.

Most people in power really do not know what life is truly like for the common man. Do you know what it is like to live from your pay check to pay check?

Where it would seem like half of your pay check is going to taxation but where is that money going? The common man is losing services but cannot afford to access the services he loses because the cost of the service has gone up.

Why has the development of rural communities stopped? Who feeds the people in the city? Where do people think the bread that you eat comes from? Where do people think that meat comes from? Someone has to raise the food? Where would our city folk be without the rural support?

Do the rural communities not deserve the same resources as the city? Why is there such differences in what is paid to our seniors and resources for our seniors?

These people have paid into the system their whole entire lives in Canada and are living at poverty line.

They deserve our care do they not?

Where is priority funding? Education? Healthcare? How are we creating new business to pay off our debt? TAXATION IS NOT A SOLUTION! People have been taxed to death and are tired of taxes going up and all people not contributing to the system.

I understand, there are people who may have it far worse...and they might have nothing I get it, as Ghandi said, I once met a man who had no shoes, then I met a man who had no feet!...however...In Canada, we have rural communities and reservations that do not have quality running water.

Kids are still reading the same books from 30 years ago! Rural communities do not have access to technology resources. There are lack of supplies and proper development of resources for the people who are living in all of these communities. Fly in or otherwise. We are having serious mental health issues with our children.

Why are educators expected to compensate for the lack of resources in education? Would you expect a surgeon to shell out of pocket for the resources needed to do their jobs?

Teachers are doing the best that they can...but resources are so limited...new funding is needed and outside resource supports are required to give our public education systems the shot of steroids it needs to meet the needs of "all" children!

Canadian students want more exposure to global culture. Students want the same opportunities as their Indigenous classmates....they hear their classmates say, I can't wait to turn 18!

Which means in the eyes of the other non-first nations children, all opportunities paid. While the rest of the students around them are not given that same opportunity.

How do we teach equality to our students if our students are not treated equally by our governments and the labels society has placed on them? Are these children superior to the rest of society that they are not given the same parameters of expectations and accountability as the other children? Are the expectations and outcomes the same?

Students do not understand why they were given their treaty rights and what that meant and the lengths that their great leaders had to go to ensure the rights of the Indigenous people.

All nations of students are not happy that they are losing their heritage as traditions are not being handed down through language, food, spiritual traditions or the like.

Students in Canada are wanting an explanation as to why they have to take a student loan or why they have to get a job to be able to attend University or Community College?

Students in Canada are wanting answers from those who were here "first", why all students aren't forced to step up and contribute back "first"?

Students want to talk openly about these issues but because of "political correctness", issues are being swept under the carpet and no one is really addressing what is really going on.

Curriculums are very dated. Students do not know the laws around them. Students want to know how to file taxes. They want to know how money works, how to get a bank loan etc. These skills that were formally taught by the home are no longer being taught and students are not knowing basic skills. They are looking to their teachers at school.

Our societies have become so capitalistic with immediate gratification that no one is forced to wait any more. No one is made to work for much, rather, they just expect things to be handed to them.

This is the problem with all of our societies where children are given things, they do not appreciate true value.

They do not understand the process because they have never been made to work to understand what went into the process. What happens on the outside because of the choices made by the adults, impacts the little people in our classrooms.

As we educators spend so much time, as supposedly "secondary", parents, we see the realities of the negative societal choices and we are then expected to create the solutions and solve the problems to educate *the little ones!*

The less responsibilities that people take these days with rearing their off spring, the more responsibility is placed on the school. Where is the line because it has been totally crossed?

These issues will not be solved by anyone but leadership to demand accountability from their children. Perhaps incentive based funding for goal achievement would be an option to consider. If you do this….then you can have this…win -win!

The people deserve to know the feeling of achievement and the feeling of taking back your personal power and defining your own success! These learning values are applied to all human beings.

All children deserve to grow up with accountable inspired leadership all around them. How many more children in our societies have to grow up re-living the negative components in any culture before accountability is demanded and changes are made?

Taxation and banking systems in the developed nations are extremely complicated to understand, with the common man not understanding where all of their money is being spent, how money is created and how the banking system operates.

Governments are forcing their people to absorb their costs but fewer revenue streams are being created to compensate or give back to the people in the way of tangible services and resources.

What do you value as a country? Where are your funding resources going to? Do you value war or do you value education and human innovation? "A nation that continues year after year to spend more on military spending then programs of social uplift is approaching spiritual death". Dr.Martin Luther KIng

If I was sick and I knocked on any hospital door, would I get treatment even if I didn't have money in my pocket? Would I be resorted to the "a" section or the "b" section? Is there equal opportunity for all?

How do you model equality to children if funding allocation is based on competition? Education is evolving and requires constant funding. If government cannot absorb the cost to give public education the shot of steroids it needs for constant development, how do you bridge the funding gap in public education?

What is your vision for your nations as leaders being fathers and mothers of all children living within the borders of your country?

What information are you feeding into the minds of your children? Children are a product of their environment and covet what they see.

Children need to be taught to think, process and apply information for themselves. They are at a disadvantage when everything is given to them. One cannot experience the feeling of personal success, which sets the standard for personal achievement, if one does not know the feeling of failure. One cannot learn anything new if they are afraid to make mistakes.

Life experience gained through trial and error builds knowledge application skills. Teach children to work for the things that they want or they will never appreciate what they have. They will always expect everything to be given to them. Give them positive incentives creating goals. If you do this...then you can have this!

Your children love boundaries and love to know where they stand. Inspire cultures of respect and not cultures of fear. To inspire others to achieve greatness, we must inspire it within ourselves. "Be the change you wish to see in the world". Mahatma Ghandi

Expect success and you will get success, however, expect failure, and that is what you will get. Rule with an iron fist and you will rule with fear. Inspire greatness and breed cultures of respect. Demonstrate what it means to succeed and how one fails gracefully. Demonstrate sportsman like conduct at all times!

"Teach how we agree to disagree. Teach how we embrace cultural diversity and the strengths of all. Unite your societies, do not divide them. Discuss the problem not the person, there is a difference!

Take care of your people first, then they will take care of others. It is the equivalent to putting the oxygen mask on your child first before you save yourself! Ensure that your economies are strong and your problems are solved before you start messing about in someone else's back yard!

Grow your societies, but do not compromise your people to turn your profits. That includes every person who is not from your religious sect or nationality!

Everyone deserves freedom and everyone deserves to know the feeling of free movement and equal opportunity regardless of language spoken and chosen book of enlightenment or passport origin.

Everyone deserves a passport and everyone deserves to have a homeland! With that in mind, your chosen book of enlightenment should be taught within in your homes. These are personal values.

The public learning forum is a place for expression of all intelligence's, all colours, creeds and thought! FOR THE EVOLUTION OF ALL OF HUMANITY". The books have provided humanity with wonderful comfort, but have also caused a lot of the problems on the planet.

I wish all people on the planet could experience the feeling of freedom like I know it. The feeling of being able to get off an airplane in more than 150 countries around the globe without having to ask permission ahead of time. That feeling of world pride that I have knowing, that my country is totally loved by the world and I can proudly walk the planet with my flag on back!

I am so very proud of that right that I have as a 4th generation born Canadian as in the spectrum of time, it was not so long ago that my family immigrated to Canada from Poland and the Ukraine. How blessed I have been to have had the opportunity to grow up with the opportunities available in Canada.

Every Canadian would agree, they wold not trade their place with anyone on the planet. We love everyone and we are the most patient, tolerant and kindest people on the planet! We truly are peacekeepers and we believe in the development of all people. At least this very proud Canadian does eh!"

My great uncle, extended family members and neighbours went to the battlefield to afford me that right. I will never forget their sacrifice and the freedoms that we have today because of their great sacrifices on the international scale, protecting our country.

"I can't imagine what that man who I grew up 200 meters down the road from me experienced when he

was in the war. I don't even want to. I had heard stories, but he wouldn't talk about it. Rumblings of having to eat rats to stay alive because he was a prisoner of war.

That is true sacrifice for your country. I salute the flag, place my hand on my heart and stand on guard every time I hear the Canadian National anthem. Thank you for my freedom"!

Celebrate the great warriors and the traditions of the past. Hold on to the beautiful spiritual traditions that served your people well. Continue to teach your children to sing and to dance.

Celebrate the bountiful harvest brought forth from the earth! Hold onto the tradition of living off the land. Embrace our mother earth and feel the joy of your loved ones energy around you.

However, it is time to change the patterns of 21st century cultures of blame. One can choose failure, or one can choose success. Demand change and accountability from your children and break this negative growth cycle.

The evolution of our children depend on it! You are the leadership in your environment. Do not expect from others what you are not prepared to do for yourself.

Chapter 4
Theoretical Physics
a Brief History in Time –Dr. Stephen Hawking

"The beginning of the universe had, of course, been discussed long before this. According to a number of early cosmologies and the Jewish/Christian/Muslim tradition, the universe started at a finite, and not very distant, time in the past. One argument for such a beginning was the feeling that it was necessary to have "First Cause" to explain the existence of the universe. (Within the universe, you always explained one event as being caused by some earlier event, but the existence of the universe itself could be explained in this way only if it had some beginning.)

Another argument was put forward by St. Augustine in his book The City of God. He pointed out that civilization is progressing and we remember who performed this deed or developed that technique. Thus man, and so also perhaps the universe, could not have been around all that long. St. Augustine accepted a date of about 5000 BC for the Creation of the universe according to the book of Genesis. (It is interesting that this is not so far from the end of the last Ice Age, about 10,000 BC, which is when archaeologists tell us that civilization really began.)

Aristotle, and most of the other Greek philosophers, on the other hand, did not like the idea of a creation because it smacked too much of divine intervention. They believed, therefore, that the human race and the world around it had existed, and would exist, forever. The ancients had already considered the argument about progress described above, and answered it by saying that there had been periodic floods or other disasters that repeatedly set the human race right back to the beginning of civilization.

The questions of whether the universe had a beginning in time and whether it is limited in space were later extensively examined by the philosopher Immanuel Kant in his monumental (and very obscure) work Critique of Pure Reason, published in 1781. He called these questions antinomies (that is, contradictions) of pure reason because he felt that there were equally compelling arguments for believing the thesis, that the universe had a beginning, and the antithesis, that it had existed forever. His argument for the thesis was that if the universe did not have a beginning, there would be an infinite period of time before any event, which he considered absurd.

The argument for the antithesis was that if the universe had a beginning, there would be an infinite period of time before it, so why should the universe begin at any one particular time? In fact, his cases for both the thesis and the antithesis are really the same argument. They are both based on his unspoken assumption that time continues back forever, whether or not the universe had existed forever. As we shall see, the concept of time has no meaning before the beginning of the universe.

This was first pointed out by St. Augustine. When asked: "What did God do before he created the universe?" Augustine didn't reply: "He was preparing Hell for people who asked such questions." Instead, he said that time was a property of the universe that God created, and that time did not exist before the beginning of the universe. When most people believed in an essentially static and unchanging universe, the question of whether or not it had a beginning was really one of metaphysics or theology.

One could account for what was observed equally well on the theory that the universe had existed forever or on the theory that it was set in motion at some finite time in such a manner as to look as though it had existed forever. But in 1929, Edwin Hubble made the landmark observation that wherever you look, distant galaxies are moving rapidly away from us.

In other words, the universe is expanding. This means that at earlier times objects would have been closer together. In fact, it seemed that there was a time, about ten or twenty thousand million years ago, when they were all at exactly the same place and when, therefore, the density of the universe was infinite. This discovery finally brought the question of the beginning of the universe into the realm of science.

Hubble's observations suggested that there was a time, called the big bang, when the universe was infinitesimally small and infinitely dense. Under such conditions all the laws of science, and therefore all ability to predict the future, would break down. If there were events earlier than this time, then they could not affect what happens at the present time. Their existence can be ignored because it would have no observational consequences. One may say that time had a beginning at the big bang, in the sense that earlier times simply would not be defined.

It should be emphasized that this beginning in time is very different from those that had been considered previously. In an unchanging universe a beginning in time is something that has to be imposed by some being outside the universe; there is no physical necessity for a beginning.

One can imagine that God created the universe at literally any time in the past. On the other hand, if the universe is expanding, there may be physical reasons why there had to be a beginning. One could still imagine that God created the universe at the instant of the big bang, or even afterwards in just such a way as to make it look as though there had been a big bang, but it would be meaningless to suppose that it was created before the big bang. An expanding universe does not preclude a creator, but it does place limits on when he might have carried out his job!" Dr. Stephen Hawking

Chapter 5

E=ME2 –Theory of VERITAS, and Time
The Law of Attraction

I *AM* the singularity. The universe has always existed and will continue to exist. The universe expands through thought. ***Time is thought in motion eternally.*** "Every thought is the equivalent to a *"big bang"* expanding the universe based on the thought that was thought. ***Every thought that has ever existed, still exists"***. Esther Hicks.

There is no death, only continued thought evolution expanding the energy of life. As sure as the sun will rise, so will you!

Welcome to planet earth! We hope that you enjoy your stay here. Everything in the universe is interconnected and is operating on a chain of frequency of vibrational energy.

Your quality of life will depend entirely on the thoughts that you think and the emotions that you feel. The two words I AM are the most important words for what you put after them, you will most certainly become. THINK YES, AND YOU WILL GET YES!

I AM the energy of your tears and I AM designed to fix you. Negative emotions are a warning bell telling you that YOU are deserving of better.

The truth will set YOU free, but it might really tick YOU off first. It might light up the energy frequency sensors of sight, sound, taste, smell, touch, and emotional internal sensors inside of your body as joy that feels just like heaven! Or it might light you up with anger, pain, feelings that don't feel that good, that feels like hell! That is negative energy.

Be aware of those feelings but don't keep thinking them for they will make your heart energy sick if you keep thinking that way all the time. You will always find relief when you change the perspective of your problem. The solution will feel a lot different than the problem.

Find the positive in your situation, and move forward. When you know what you don't want, it brings you closer to knowing what you do want. Making mistakes is how you will learn.

Think how did that thought make you feel? The resonance of the frequency of the thought will connect with the internal sensors and do what the thought wills it. However, this is only possible if one believes it is possible.

Universal energy is inclusionary, pure, positive well-being and is only love which is why it feels so great. Your mission in this life is to go forth in life evolving your thought through collecting experience.

Sometimes your heart will sing the tune of really happy songs and other times, your heart will sing the frequency of sad songs. You will tell by the way that you feel.

Human beings are not created in the likeness of "GOD", rather they are made from the same infinite source energy that operates the same laws of the universe in which the universe was created. **This source energy is not a separate entity outside of the realm from human beings rather it is the same chain of energy.**

Nothing on the planet can disassociate from it, plants, animals, human beings and nature are all extensions of source energy. The law of attraction, which is the most powerful natural law of the universe, currently portrayed by society as being "new age thought", is not "new thought", at all.

Hundreds of years ago the Law of Attraction was first thought to have been taught to man through the immortal Buddha, who wanted it to be known that 'what you have become is what you have thought' – a belief that is deeply intrinsic with the Law of Attraction. With the spread of this concept to western culture also came the term 'Karma', a belief that is popular throughout numerous societies.

Throughout history, a great many women and men who have left their mark on this world have shown the Law of Attraction to be one of the greatest powers on earth; with many well-loved poets, artists, scientists and great thinkers such as Shakespeare, Blake, Emerson, Newton, and Beethoven all conveying this message through their many works.

The main principles of the Law of Attraction can also be discovered in the teachings of many civilizations and religious groups. An example – in the proverbs 23:7, it reads 'As a man Thinketh and so is he'. Proof of praise for the Laws of Attraction can be uncovered throughout the ages; all recorded and taught in different ways, but still there for all of humanity to find and many who have understood it. As Winston Churchill said "You create your own universe as you go along".

Once we have come to understand the astounding possibilities that life has to offer us, we can also come to realize that we are like artists – creating pictures of our intended life and then making choices and taking actions that will realize what we envisaged. Life is a blank canvas of possibility; you are in control of what the finished picture could look like.

The Law of Attraction really is that simple – no catches. All laws of nature are completely perfect and the Law of Attraction is no exception.

The "New Thought" movement grew out of the teachings of Phineas Quimby in the early 19th century. Although he never used the words "law of attraction", his basic premise was similar, although restricted only to the health care field: "the trouble is in the mind, for the body is only the house for the mind to dwell in, and we put a value on it according to its worth.

Therefore if your mind has been deceived by some invisible enemy into a belief, you have put it into the form of a disease, with or without your knowledge. By my theory or truth I come in contact with your enemy, and restore you to your health and happiness.

This I do partly mentally and partly by talking till I correct the wrong impressions and establish the Truth, and the Truth is the cure".

In 1877, the term 'law of attraction' appeared in print for the first time in a book written by Helena Blavatsky. By the end of the 19th century the term was being used by New Thought authors such as Prentice Mulford and Ralph Trine, but for them the law of attraction not only affected health but every other aspect of our lives.

The 20th century saw a surge in interest in the subject with many books being written about it, amongst those authors are Napoleon Hill and William D. Wattles. Other teachers of the law of attraction are, W. Clement Stone, Dale Carnegie, Earl Nightingale, Neville Godard and 21st century teachers, Wayne Dyer, Louise Hay, Esther and

Jerry Hicks, Joe Vitale, Deepak Chopra, John Demartini, Oprah Winfrey, Jack Canfield, John Assaraf, Brian Tracy, Anthony Robbins, Bob Proctor, Zig Ziglar, Sandy Gallagher, Lisa Nichols and Vishen Lakhiani to name a few.

Chapter 6

Man's Greatest Achievement
Changing the Non-Physical to Physical $E = mc^2$

"Nicola Tesla imagined a world where new scientific discoveries, rather than war, would become a priority for humanity. Today the most civilized countries of the world spend a maximum of their income on war and a minimum on education. The twenty-first century will reverse this order. It will be more glorious to fight against ignorance than to die on the field of battle. The discovery of a new scientific truth will be more important than the squabbles of diplomats. Even the newspapers of our own day are beginning to treat scientific discoveries and the creation of fresh philosophical concepts as news. The newspapers of the twenty-first century will give a mere " stick " in the back pages to accounts of crime or political controversies, but will headline on the front pages the proclamation of a new scientific hypothesis.

Man's greatest achievement, according to Tesla, which was published on July 6, 1930 in New York American states that when a child is born its sense-organs are brought in contact with the outer world. The waves of sound, heat, and light beat upon its feeble body, its sensitive nerve-fibres quiver, the muscles contract and relax in obedience: a gasp, a breath, and in this act a marvellous little engine, of inconceivable delicacy and complexity of construction, unlike any on earth, is hitched to the wheel-work of the Universe.

The little engine labours and grows, performs more and more involved operations, becomes sensitive to ever subtler influences and now there manifests itself in the fully developed being - Man - a desire mysterious, inscrutable and irresistible: to imitate nature, to create, to work himself the wonders he perceives. Inspired in this task he searches, discovers and invents, designs and constructs, and enriches with monuments of beauty, grandeur and awe, the star of his birth.

He descends into the bowels of the globe to bring forth its hidden treasures and to unlock its immense imprisoned energies for its use. He invades the dark depths of the ocean and the azure regions of the sky. He peers into the innermost nook sand recesses of molecular structure and lays bare to his gaze worlds infinitely remote. He subdues and puts to his service the fierce, devastating spark of Prometheus, the titanic forces of the waterfall, the wind and the tide.

He tames the thundering bolt of Jove and annihilates time and space. He makes the great Sun itself his obedient toiling slave. Such is the power and might that the heavens reverberate and the whole earth trembles by the mere sound of his voice. What has the future in store for this strange being, born of a breath, of perishable tissue, yet immortal, with his powers fearful and divine? What magic will be wrought by him in the end? What is to be his greatest deed, his crowning achievement? Long ago he recognized that all perceptible matter comes from a primary substance, of a tenuity beyond conception and filling all space - the Akasha or luminiferous ether - which is acted upon by the life-giving Prana or creative force, calling into existence, in never ending cycles, all things and phenomena.

The primary substance, thrown into infinitesimal whirls of prodigious velocity, becomes gross matter; the force subsiding, the motion ceases and matter disappears, reverting to the primary substance. Can Man control this grandest, most awe-inspiring of all processes in nature? Can he harness her inexhaustible energies to perform all their functions at his bidding, more still - can he so refine his means of control as to put them in operation simply by the force of his will?

If he could do this he would have powers almost unlimited and supernatural. At his command, with but a slight effort on his part, old worlds would disappear and new ones of his planning would spring into being. He could fix, solidify and preserve the ethereal shapes of his imagining, the fleeting visions of his dreams. He could express all the creations of his mind, on any scale, in forms concrete and imperishable. He could alter the size of this planet, control its seasons, and guide it along any path he might choose through the depths of the Universe. He could make planets collide and produce his suns and stars, his heat and light. He could srcinate and develop life in all its infinite forms.

To create and annihilate material substance, cause it to aggregate in forms according to his desire, would be the supreme manifestation of the power of Man's mind, his most complete triumph over the physical world, his crowning achievement which would place him beside his creator and fulfil his ultimate destiny." Nicola Tesla

"$E = mc^2$"

German-born physicist Albert Einstein's theory of relativity demonstrates that the increased relativistic mass (m) of a body comes from the energy of motion of the body—that is, its kinetic energy (E)—divided by the speed of light squared (c^2). This equation expresses the fact that mass and energy are the same physical entity and can be changed into each other.

Einstein also theorized that everything is energy, match the frequency of the reality you want and you cannot help but get that reality, the imagination is everything, it is the preview of life's coming attractions.

Through a variety of systematic problem solving processes such as creative visualization, Visioneering, creative meditation and visual motor rehearsal where one visualizes the end result and through the frequency of emotion based on the thought that was thought, the energy from the non-physical is transformed to physical manifestation turning thoughts to things.

Dr. Denis Waitley, Ph. D, has trained both NASA astronauts and Olympic athletes, using Visual Motor Rehearsal. He would hook the athletes up to biofeedback equipment, and have the athletes run their event only in their mind. He found that the same muscles fired in the same sequence, when they were running the event in their mind, as when they were running it on track.

He determined that the mind can't distinguish whether you're really doing something, or if it's just a practice. He believes if you go there in the mind, you will go there in the body.

Thoughts emit a frequency of energy that can be measured. Much like vibration made from playing musical chords on an instrument, our emotional guidance system operates in the same way reading the energy frequency.

Based on the frequency of the thought, through the law

of attraction, human beings create life experience, both positive and negative. The universe is inclusionary electrical energy, positive = positive, negative = negative. Like attracts like!

The energy created by the mind of human beings is much like a swirling vortex of energy. The physical senses of sight, taste, touch, smell and hearing are interpreters of that frequency of energy vibration.

The feeling in the chest located between the solar plexus, known as the emotional guidance system, or the 6th sense of INTUITION or Energy in Motion as emotion. This is VERITAS, Latin translation, truth. Vibration Energy Reading Intuition Truth's Accurate Sensor. It is a wiser you that remembers what it feels like to be connected to universal energy, or God, source, the ethers, your higher self, or the 99 other names one wants describe "God"(yourself).

This JUDGEMENT indicator is human's G.P.S (or God's Perfect Sensor). This is a sophisticated instrument given to humans as a mechanism to tell them 100% at any moment in time what is right or wrong.

This internal guidance indicator lets people know what energy frequency they are emitting or attracting based on correlation of thoughts that are being thought and emotions being felt. Anything other than positive emotion and thought does not feel good.

This "physics of musical notes" indicator measures the frequency reading the energy emitted through the bodies frequency interpreters of the senses, much like a global positioning system letting the body know if it is in balance or out of balance.

Negative emotion and contrast is designed as a warning bell bringing a person closer to preferred positive experience based on the standard of joy, knowledge, love, empowerment, appreciation and gratitude.

Figure 1.3

VERITAS Energy Tuner / Correlating Feeling

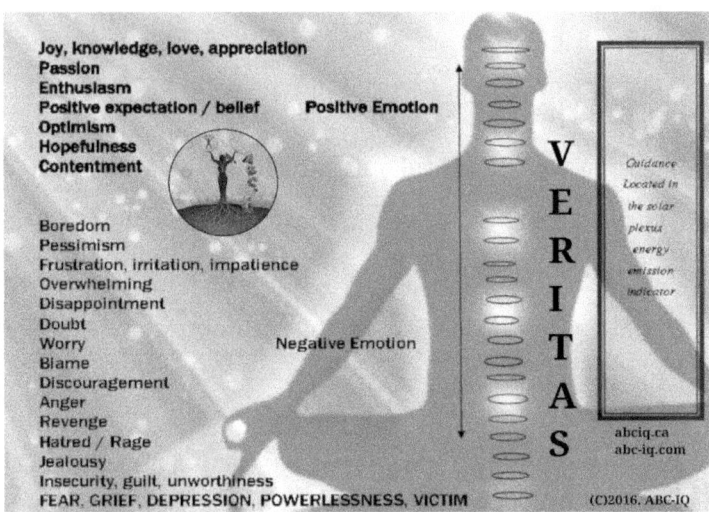

Energy from the body is released in the form of tears, anger, happiness, joy, when the body becomes overloaded with negative or positive energy. Contrast and making mistakes is designed to support humans learn knowledge application skills.

Based on the intensity of emotional experience, we retain information and remember the experience based on the way that we felt. Negative emotion and experience is designed to carry the message at all times, you are deserving of better. Reaching for a better feeling thought will bring a feeling of relief and support with finding the solution.

The internal guidance system is an indicator letting the body know if it is in balance or out of balance. The more out of balance our body system is, the more stress is created in the body until it eventually attracts sickness. Negative emotion, the warning bell in the body, causes discord, which eventually causes stress, the root cause of sickness. "A body that is at ease, cannot live with dis-ease". Esther Hicks

Massachusetts General Hospital (MGH) conducted a study with participants in a relaxation-response-focused training program examining relaxation response techniques such as meditation, yoga and prayer. These practises reduce the need for healthcare services by 43%.

Previous studies have shown that eliciting the relaxation response — a physiologic state of deep rest — not only relieves stress and anxiety, but also affects physiologic factors such as blood pressure, heart rate, and oxygen consumption.

Research conducted at the Institute for Technology Assessment and the Benson-Henry Institute (BHI) for Mind Body Medicine, found that individuals in the relaxation response program used few health care services in one year after tier participation in the preceding year. "If every eight year old child on the planet was taught meditation, we would eliminate violence from the world in one generation". Dalai Lama

The Mind – Neuroscience / Neuroplasticity / Mind Science Positive Psychology I AM Affirmations

I AM ARE TWO OF THE MOST IMPORTANT WORDS FOR WHAT YU PUT AFTER THEM, YOU WILL BECOME.

The mind is programmed like a computer. It has its own software which helps you to organize your thinking, actions and behaviour. If you have a behaviour that you want to change, it is a matter of re training, conditioning and re-programming. Most problems stem from the same root causes – negative thought running through the mind.

Neuro science research supports the idea that your brain remains adaptable throughout your lifetime. Each person has the power to change his or her brain for the better – this is called self-directed neuroplasticity.

This means that a person can facilitate changes in thinking (beliefs and attitudes), emotions (mindfulness and resilience) and behaviour creating new and healthy habits. Healthy habits forming mind body medicine such as mindfulness, meditation, self-awareness, self-motivation, resilience, optimism and self-efficiency.

Neuroplasticity refers to the ability of the adult brain to generate and integrate new brain cells (neurons) and remodel pre-existing neural circuits demonstrating that it is possible to change the state of mind from a negative to a positive state.

Chapter 7

Socialization / what is Culture?

Expressions of identity through the arts typically defines culture. However, culture, is also the methods in which systems thinking of environments function. Culture can also be defined as learned patterns of behavior that can be changed.

With globalization and modernization, it is highly unlikely that there are any societies on the planet that exist in total isolation and are being integrated to some extent, into the global economy. Every person on the planet is impacted by thought and systems thinking of other cultures.

Culture is the beliefs, values, habit, and material objects shared by a definite group of people. Culture is a form of living that people have in common. Our culture is reflected in what we wear to work, when and what we consume, and how we invest our recreation time.

Culture brings the circumstance within which our lives become significant, based on standards of success, beauty, and goodness.

Some cultures value competition, while others emphasize collaboration. Culture impacts virtually every aspect of our lives. Culture is not innate; human beings develop culture. Culture incorporates a set of principles and traditions transmitted from generation to generation, yet for the reason that human beings have created it, culture is pliable and subject to change.

Human culture is linked to the biological evolution of human beings. The creation of culture became probable only after the brain size of our early ancestors increased, allowing humans to build their natural background for themselves.

Human beings are creative by nature, they have developed diverse, or different, ways of life. Cultural multiplicity is the result of geographical location, religious beliefs, and lifestyles. Culture consists of symbols, attaching significance to objects and habits.

Language is the most crucial expression of cultural symbolism. Sharing beliefs, thoughts, and feelings with others is the starting point of culture. Language is the most important signifier of cultural transmission. Language allows human beings to transmit culture not only in the present, but in addition from past to future generations. Language is evidence of our humanity.

Linguistic anthropologists, Edward Sapir and Benjamin Whorf, work emphasizes the language that we speak actually determines the reality that we experience. The Sapir-Whorf speculation states that we know the world only in terms of what our language brings, that language shapes culture as a whole.

For example, while the English language has only one word for "snow," the Inuit language has different words that explain different forms of snow. This happens because distinguishing between, for example, falling snow and drifting snow is so crucial to the life of the Inuit.

While it can be true that language shapes culture, it is possibly equally true that culture shapes language. For example, the use of computers has led to new words and phrases in the language.

Words such as, "Google", "Facebook", YouTube, "gigabyte" and "RAM" (random access memory), while commonplace in English today, didn't exist 50 years ago.

As more and more countries become technologically advanced, new words and phrases will in addition become part of their languages. So language and culture are interrelated, and changes in either one are probable to result in changes in the other.

Chapter 8

East – West – Structure of Culture

How People Think - Psychology

Eastern and western societies experience discord integrating thought, bridging the "energy gap" of thought that has originated outside of their environments, integrating some practice and not others.

Eastern societies are group thinking societies, hierarchal in structure, with a top down leadership approaches to life while western democratic societies and processes designed around the individual, democracy and consensus building.

Thought processes are on the opposite ends of the spectrum with the east being a group thinking mentality and the west being an individual thinking society.

Children in the east are raised to "problem solve" with the thought process of, how will my choice impact my community, family and then self. In the west, children are raised to "problem solve" with the thought of how will my choice impact ME with little regard for family and broader community.

Eastern children demonstrate high levels of emotional and social intelligence, due to the structure of society and the importance of maintaining positive relationships.

Hospitality is celebrated through offerings of cultural food and drink. These practices, social and oral traditions are enduring and are still prevalent in societal family and business cultures.

It is customary to always offer one something to drink, welcomed with dates or traditional coffee or tea.

One demonstrates respect for their elders through formalized greetings. Children are taught from very young to respect their mothers, fathers, grand-fathers, grand-mothers as well as all members of their extended family and broader community.

Social Experience and Human Development

The importance of social experience is palpable in the lack of human development features of socially isolated children, particularly, if early childhood is devoid of social experience, the child may fail to develop usual language skills prominent to restrictions in other social learning.

Sigmund Freud believed that people learn the cultural values and norms which make up a component of the personality which he called, the superego. If the superego didn't develop the right way, the person would have a very complicated time functioning in society.

Jean Piaget believed that human development is the result of both biological maturation and going up social experiences. George Herbert Mead believed that an individual's social experience was the primary determinant of individual identity, which Mead called "the self." To Mead, the self-contained two dimensions: the "I," which was partly guided from within; and the "me," which was partly guided by the reactions of others.

Charles Horton Cooley in addition emphasized the importance of the reactions of others to the creating self-concept. He used the phrase, "looking-glass self," to explain how our conception of ourselves is influenced by our perceptions of how others answer to us. Louise Hay deems this approach as "mirror work" with one self-reflecting to get to the root cause of the emotional problem causing sickness in the body. Self – talk either makes a person, or completely breaks them.

Socialization: Family, School, Peers, and the Mass Media

We start the process of socialization within the circumstance of our family. The family has primary importance in shaping a child's attitudes and behavior for the reason that it brings the circumstance in which the first and most long-lasting intimate social relationships are educated. This relationship represents the child's entire social world, the family in addition determines the child's initial social status and identity in terms of race, religion, social class, and gender.

While the family offers the child intimate social relationships, the school offers more aim social relationships. School is a social institution, and as such, has direct obligation for instilling in, or teaching, the individual the information, aptitudes, and values that society takes in consideration important for social life. In school, children learn the aptitudes of interpersonal interaction. They learn to share, to take turns, and to compromise with their peers.

The peer group exerts a most strong social influence on the child. The peer group is composed of status equals; that is, all children within a given peer group are the same age and come from the same social status.

A child must earn his/her social position within the peer group; this position doesn't come easily, as it does in the family. Interaction with a peer group loosens the child's bonds to the family; it brings both a substitute model for habit and new social norms and values. To become fully socialized, children must discover how to get involved with the conflicting views and values of each and every one of the people who are crucial in their lives. These people are called "significant others."

Feeding the Mind – NEGATIVE Media

The mass media consists of television, newspapers, internet, radio, and magazines; and signifies of communication which are directed toward an extensive audience in society. The mass media, specifically television, has appreciable influence on the process of socialization.

Studies completed by Rand demonstrate that people spend an a great deal of their time watching television, and the violent content of multiple television programs is believed to be a contributing circumstance in aggressive habit.

Media is flooding society with negative culture instilling sickness, intolerance, hatred and capitalism into those who watch. Through the law of attraction, attention to any subject multiplies it. There is a war on terrorism that is just getting bigger! Cultures of peace are not being promoted, rather the opposite is resulting. This is also applied to teen age pregnancy, divorce, sickness and every other facet that impacts the human life experience.

Separation of Theology and the State

WE ARE ALL HUMAN!

Information control, lack of free speech and imposed through governmental control of information does not allow for individuals to grow and evolve to full potential thus impeding in the basic right for all humans to choose what is acceptable and not acceptable for their bodies.

Societal laws are formulated around religious books imposing religious law on all people in all walks of life based on the "supreme" word of "GOD" based on what was written thousands of years ago. These laws and books have not taken into account the changing faces of our societies to allow for free thought, freedom to choose and societal evolution.

Although, very much needed to support order within society, the basis of law is still on theology formulating the moral compass as to what is right and wrong.

Not all people are Christian, Muslim, Jewish, Buddhist and so on. Separation of church and state does not fully exist. If it did, one would not be forced to swear on a bible in the court of law as the Bible / Quran being the supreme word representing all people in western / eastern judicial systems, women would be free to control their own bodies, abortion, divorce, "suicide", and assisted death would not carry such a stigma, priests and nuns would be free to marry, eat, wear and cohabitate with whom they choose regardless of sexual orientation. *It is my body, it is my right to decide....*

Equality by definition in the east and western societies means two different things. In western society, equality means just that, equal division. Equality in the east, however, is defined based on roles of male and female and gender. *"With male being treated as the "superior", head of the family and decision maker and woman assuming all roles and responsibilities within the home. The women in the east have the responsibility of protecting the families "honour" while men have little accountability. This might be the reason why change in the "old world" is slow in coming. In order for societies to change, it must be embraced, by all.*

Eastern thought processes are inherently not democratic, rather hierarchical with leader (father, husband, brother) having more power and influence over all matters. Females viewed as the weaker sex, are required to seek the permission from the male for free movement. Females / males are not permitted to be in the company of men / women unless one is related, married or in a working situation.

Pre-marital sexual relations are illegal. Women who find themselves with child out of wedlock are jailed and deported. Marriages are arranged, with children marrying relatives or "friends", of the family. People are not free to marry whom they choose as the state / law / culture does not permit "infidel" infiltration".

There are many allegations from the west against the east and vice versa. There is a lack of respect for human rights and democracy with dealing with these issues. Peace will never come to the Middle Eastern region when it looks down the barrel of a gun.

The world benefits a great deal from unrest within the Middle Eastern region. It is to the advantage of many that wars continue as weapons are needed and new sources of oil revenues are required to sustain economies.

Politics of fear instilled in the people through the media about the people of the East is out of control. Every Muslim from the Eastern world is labelled in the media when any negative escalates in the west, however, this is not the case with the label of "Christian" or "Jewish", to offenders in the west.

The East does not understand the western concept of democracy. This is an entire region of people, who have no idea what it feels like to be free. *"Free thought, within defined parameters of what is acceptable and not acceptable is contradictory to the foundations of every education system which promotes expansion of the individual to choose"*.

There will always be a continental divide in thought between the east and west, in terms of process, thought and mentality, however, people are people, regardless of where you reside on the planet. All people should be given equal opportunity of free movement and be given the basic fundamental right to choose.

One will never understand the situation of another until you experience it for yourself. The people of the east are as deserving of living a life of peace and prosperity as the people of the west.

The people should be afforded the same rights to defend themselves, their way of life and protect themselves from threat to their homeland.

In the same way that the western developed countries can defend themselves and their borders, the people of the east should be afforded that same right and be left alone to live in peace to continue practising their way of life.

Democratization and modernization are two different things. However, one cannot exist without the other. Free thought is the basis of the creation of the charter of rights and freedoms that formulates governmental laws of most societies.

This thought, with globalization, cannot help but become widespread. The east cannot implement processes of modernization without implementing the foundations of thought within the process, it is contradictory and reform is required for long term success.

What the east needs to realize is that modernization and westernization are two different things, a society can become modernized and not westernized.

A final word…. *"It is ok to give up control and let the*

oppressed go free! Your environments are developed not only by the support of your "nationals", your countries got where they are because of the diversity of all people in the borders. A thank you goes a long way!

What might a "servant less" society look like if the "nations" "national" people were forced to do the work of the "help"? Perhaps cultures of responsibility would be developed?

Equal contribution and opportunity....I AM...Just a thought ☺

Chapter 9

Conclusion

Life is meant to be positive! When we are born, we come to the planet with a clean slate. Everything that we learn is a result of cultural influence around us. Beliefs are thoughts that we keep thinking based on our chosen life experience.

Our thoughts and life experience is influenced and formulated based on the culture of the environment around us.

Problems cannot be solved using the same thinking in which they were created. Humans must change their perception and see the world through seeking solution by utilizing different thought and a different vantage point.

The solution feels much different than the problem. How did that thought make you feel? FEEL Solution through finding a better feeling thought! Seek joy and remember the feeling!

If a person wants to change life experience, they will

have to change the way that they think and perceive situations. Through contrast by gaining life experience acquiring knowledge, mankind makes choices based on experience to choose wanted and unwanted life experience.

Contrast leads a person to make the next choice for what life experience is wanted. Memory is retained based on the intensity of the emotion felt in the experience.

Words provide a basis for learning. Experience of applying words to our life experience creates knowledge application. Words do not teach, applied life experience does!

21st century, knowledge based global economies require self- starters, creatively skilled learners who are culturally diverse, tolerant, well informed, communicative and empathetic while being open to understanding global culture.

Exposure to new thought and new life experience through travel brings exposure to cultural diversity allowing broadened perspectives.

We live in a world of duality. One cannot exist without the other. "Human beings are energy beings that are either physically or non-physically focused". Esther Hicks

Death of the physical human vessel results in energy leaving the human body and returning back to non-physical energy, still present in the universe but operating from a different vantage point.

There is no separation as they are a part of the same positive energy spectrum of physical or non-physical focused energy.

There is no darkness, only absence of light. The presence of heaven or hell as interpreted in theology, is the equivalent to what humans live each and every day on the planet. Joy, love, appreciation, passion, positive emotion and gratitude energy is the equivalent of heaven, negative emotion, grief, pain, and sorrow, negative emotion is the equivalent of hell, opposite polarities of the same spectrum.

"Universal energy is inclusion based, constant and evolving electrical positive energy. Humans create life experience based on thoughts that they think. Every thought is the equivalent to a "big bang" resulting in physical manifestation of life experience" Abraham-Hicks. Time is thought energy in motion eternally, it does not stop.

Every human being re-emerges as and joins the ranks of pure positive energy. Still present in the universe, however, operating at a different frequency of energy vibration. One must tune into that energy as it is pure and positive. One accesses this energy when you are operating at that frequency.

Our loved ones energy is all around us, now we interpret them with different energy frequency sensors in our body! They are what we classify as our "intuition" collective consciousness. "Your soul" as energy that continues to "light you up" and operates the entire universe. They are thought!

The cycle of evolution of life will continue as the sun continues to rise. Only when the sun continues to stop shining, will life cease to remain on the planet.

We are all interconnected universal energy. All of

humanity thinks thought. That is universal truth. That is VERITAS. There is no death, only the constant cycle of life. It is just as easy to choose a positive thought as a negative thought.

In the words of Joh Fitzgerald Kennedy, "We observe today not a victory of party but a celebration of freedom--symbolizing an end as well as a beginning--signifying renewal as well as change. For I have sworn before you and Almighty God the same solemn oath our forbears prescribed nearly a century and three-quarters ago. The world is very different now. For man holds in his mortal hands the power to abolish all forms of human poverty and all forms of human life. And yet the same revolutionary beliefs for which our forebears fought are still at issue around the globe--the belief that the rights of man come not from the generosity of the state but from the hand of God".

"And so, my fellow Americans: ask not what your country can do for you--ask what you can do for your country. My fellow citizens of the world: ask not what America will do for you, but what together we can do for the freedom of man"".

We learn, we grow, we rebuild and we begin again. We have no choice but to continue. That's evolution. We learn from pain, accept the responsibility and move on to create new knowledge. Love is all that there is!

Let us remove the labels of society and start treating one another as human beings. Our world deserves to know what it would feel like to live in peace!

The universe is an untapped energy source! Let us give the negative energy a rain check and let our researchers explore alternative free energies of positive unlimited energy of the sun and grow our economies and our people organically.

Let us inspire one another and in the words of American President, Barak Obama and think "YES WE CAN". What does it matter whose book everyone is reading? It is all thought!

We are all interconnected energy beings after all! We all just want to be happy! One small step of changing your thought from negative to positive will impact your entire life! "That is one small step for man, and one giant leap for mankind"! Neil Armstrong

Wake up each day and look at yourself in the mirror and love yourself, thinking, what is the best thing that can happen to me today? This is going to be the best day of my life! I am going to rock it today!

I AM………what goes at the end of this sentence…you decide! You are the master of your own life! The master piece that you are creating is you"! YOU ARE TRUTH!

Dance with life to find your joy!

Bibliography – Key Reading

Aboulafia, Mitchell, "George Herbert Mead", *The Stanford Encyclopedia of Philosophy* (Fall 2016 Edition), Edward N. Zalta (ed.), URL = <http://plato.stanford.edu/archives/fall2016/entries/mead/>.

Albert Einstein, "The Ultimate Quotable Einstein" Princeton University Press. Princeton, New Jersey, 2011.

Bob Proctor, (You Were born Rich), TAG Publishing LLC (June 26 2014)

Brian Tracy, "Speak to Win How to Present with Power in Any Situation". American Management Association, 2008.

Daniel Goleman, "Emotional Intelligence – Why It Can Matter More Than IQ. Bantam Books, 1997.

Daniel Goleman, "Social Intelligence". Bantam; Reprint edition (July 31, 2007)

Daniel G. Amen, (Magnificent Mind at Any Age)". Random House (2008)

David Niven, "100 Simple Secrets of Happy People". Harper Collins, (2000)

Deepak Chopra, "Seven Spiritual Laws of Success". New World Library / Amber-Allen Publishing (November 9, 1994)

Edgar Schein, "Organizational Culture and Leadership", John Wiley & Sons, March 24, 1995 - 2006.

Eugene Bardach, "A Practical Guide for Policy Analysis: The Eightfold Path to More Effective Problem Solving". 2012

Esther and Jerry Hicks, "Ask and it is given," The Law of Attraction - USA – Hay house Inc. – 2004- Vol.1.

Esther and Jerry Hicks, "Daily Planning Calendar and Study Group Workbook". U.S.A – Abraham Hicks

Publications, First Edition, November 1996.

Esther and Jerry Hicks, "The Essential Law of Attraction Collection". U.S.A – Hay House, First Edition, September 2013.

Esther and Jerry Hicks, "Getting into the Vortex, Guided Meditations". U.S.A – Hay House, First Edition 2010.

Howard Gardner, Frames of Mind, Basic Books; Third Edition (2011)

Jack Canfield, "The Success Principles". William Morrow Paperbacks; Reprint edition (December 26, 2006)

Jack Canfield, "Coaching for Breakthrough Success". McGraw-Hill Education; 1 edition (July 16, 2013)

John F. Kennedy Inaugural Address Transcription courtesy of the John F. Kennedy Presidential Library and Museum. http://www.ourdocuments.gov/doc.php?doc=91&page=transcript

John Gottman, Raising an Emotionally Intelligent Child. Simon and Schuster Paperbacks (1997)

Joseph Murphy, "The Subconscious Mind". Wilder Publications (November 24, 2008)

Louise Hay, "Heal Your Life". Hay House; 2 edition (January 1, 1984)

Kellog Foundation, Systems Thinking Logic Model, (2014)

Napoleon Hill, "Think and Grow Rich", the 21st Century Edition, Revised and Updated. 2004.

Napoleon Hill, "The Laws of Success", Wilder Publications (January 17, 2011)

Nicola Tesla, http://www.smithsonianmag.com/history/nikola-teslas-amazing-predictions-for-the-21st-century-26353702/#GZI5Yyc8mBSjtYg4.99

Give the gift of Smithsonian magazine for only $12!
http://bit.ly/1cGUiGv
Pam Robins, Harvey B. Alvy, The Principal's Companion. Second Edition. Corwin Press, (2003).
Paul McKenna, "Instant Confidence". Bantam Press (16 Jan, 2006)
Physics of Music.
http://www.phy.mtu.edu/~suits/notefreqs.html (2016)
Rhonda Byrne, "The Secret": Atria Books/Beyond Words; 1st Atria Books/Beyond Words Hardcover edition (November 28, 2006
Sarah McKay, "Neuroscience Newsletter": Dr. Sarah McKay Australia 2016.
Shelley Chuchmuch, "The Impacts of Education and Modernization on the Arab Word". Michigan State University, United States of America, 2005.
Steve Jobs, "Stanford University Commencement Address". 2005
Steven Covey, "Principle Centred Leadership"
Steven Covey, "Seven Habits of Highly Effective People".
Stephen Hawking, (A Brief History in Time), Bantam; 01 edition (1 Mar. 1989)
Sociological Differences
http://sociology.about.com/od/Sociology101/tp/Major-Sociological-Frameworks.htm
Sigmund Freud – Simple Psychology
http://www.simplypsychology.org/Sigmund-Freud.html
Stahl JE, Dossett ML, LaJoie AS, Denninger JW, Mehta DH, Goldman R, et al. (2015) Relaxation Response and Resiliency Training and Its Effect on Healthcare Resource Utilization. PLoS ONE 10(10): e0140212. doi:10.1371/journal.pone.0140212
Wattles, Wallace D. The Science of Getting Rich. Tarcher. 2007 SBN-10: 1585426016. ISBN 978-1-58542-

601-0.
Foreign Affairs https://www.foreignaffairs.com/ (2016)
https://youtu.be/U1Qt6a-vaNM JFK to 911 Everything is a Rich Man's Trick
Institute for the Study of Globalization and Covert politics https://isgp-studies.com/kay-griggs-colonel-george-griggs-child-sexual-abuse-military
Physics of Musical Notes http://www.phy.mtu.edu/~suits/notefreqs.html
Fact Check Thrive Movement - http://www.thrivemovement.com/websites-global-domination-agenda-resource-tree

ABOUT THE AUTHOR

Shelley D. Chuchmuch resides in Manitoba Canada. She travels internationally and nationally providing Mind Science training and development seminars, talks, and consulting services utilizing positive psychology strategies building 21st century cultures of success.

www.ingramcontent.com/pod-product-compliance
Lightning Source LLC
LaVergne TN
LVHW051833080426
835512LV00018B/2844